Romeo and Juliet

ROMEO AND JULIET

A Guide to the Play

JAY L. HALIO

Greenwood Guides to Shakespeare

Greenwood Press
Westport, Connecticut • London

Library of Congress Cataloging-in-Publication Data

Halio, Jay L.
    Romeo and Juliet : a guide to the play / Jay L. Halio.
       p. cm. — (Greenwood guides to Shakespeare)
    Includes bibliographical references and index.
    ISBN 0–313–30089–5 (alk. paper)
    1. Shakespeare, William, 1564–1616.   Romeo and Juliet.
    2. Tragedy. I. Title. II. Series.
    PR2831.H28   1998
    822.3′3—dc21   98–22907

British Library Cataloguing in Publication Data is available.

Library of Congress Catalog Card Number: 98–22907
ISBN: 0–313–30089–5

First published in 1998

Greenwood Press, 88 Post Road West, Westport, CT 06881
An imprint of Greenwood Publishing Group, Inc.

Printed in the United States of America

The paper used in this book complies with the
Permanent Paper Standard issued by the National
Information Standards Organization (Z39.48-1984).

10 9 8 7 6 5 4 3 2 1

For Elise Goodman

CONTENTS

PREFACE

When the Bodleian Library recovered its original First Folio (1623) of William Shakespeare's plays, which it had previously replaced with the Third Folio (1664/1665), the most well-thumbed pages, which clearly left their mark on the volume, were those of *Romeo and Juliet.* Oxford University undergraduates (then as now) presumably found this play, among all the others, extremely moving and perhaps relevant to their own thoughts and feelings about life and love. Certainly in our own time the play has retained its enormous appeal among the young; hence, in America it has usefully replaced *Julius Caesar* in many schools as the play pupils read as their first serious introduction to Shakespeare's works. On the stage it rivals *Hamlet* as the most frequently produced in our time, and, given an adequate cast and appropriate staging, it is almost always a box office success.

The reasons for the appeal of *Romeo and Juliet* are not hard to determine. Apart from its exquisite poetry, its characters, themes, dramatic structure, and historical context (all of which are treated in the chapters that follow) provide an unending source of fascination for both young and old. Yet it is quite different in important ways from anything Shakespeare wrote before or after. In some ways it is, as the English scholar H. B. Charlton remarked, an "experimental tragedy." In fact, it hardly begins as a tragedy at all, despite the violent quarrel that breaks out in the first scene. Many elements in the dialogue and in the action combine to suggest a comedy, the warnings of the first Chorus, or Prologue, notwithstanding. In the first scenes Shakespeare indulged his penchant for comic dialogue, which he had found so successful in his earlier plays dealing with love and sex, such as *The Taming of the Shrew* and *Love's Labour's Lost.* But it seems that he was interested now in moving in another direction, altering the course of comedy to the darker mode of tragedy. Why?

Shakespeare had written tragedies before. *Titus Andronicus* was his first venture into that mode, although it really belongs to the subgenre called "revenge tragedy." As such, it was the precursor to *Hamlet,* which changed the course of revenge tragedy in Elizabethan drama. Shakespeare had also dealt with tragedy in *Richard*

II, the history play written very close in time to the composition of *Romeo and Juliet,* and before that, in quite other ways, he had touched on tragedy in *Richard III.* He was still a long way from the great tragedies of his later years; but from further experiments in plays like *King John,* he continued to learn more and more about the nature of his medium and the ways he could shape it for his own purposes.

We can only speculate as to why he was moved to combine in so flagrant a fashion the two modes of comedy and tragedy in *Romeo and Juliet.* Some scholars have supposed that the death of Shakespeare's only son, Hamnet, may have led him to think of how a potentially happy outcome could so swiftly turn otherwise (see, for example, Julia Kristeva's views discussed in Chapter 7). We will probably never know whether this is true or not, and certainly Shakespeare went on soon after Hamnet's death to write his greatest comedies, the *Henry IV* plays and the so-called Joyous Comedies (*Much Ado about Nothing, As You Like It,* and *Twelfth Night*) before once again tackling the genre of tragedy. But even in a play like *Much Ado,* a darker side of life emerges, and luck and circumstance as much as anything help to avert disaster. From almost the beginning, the close conjunction of comedy and tragedy seems to have fascinated the dramatist. For instance, in *The Comedy of Errors* Shakespeare altered his source, framing the action with the potentially tragic catastrophe threatening Egeon. What is it that makes for the different outcomes? This is the question that Shakespeare seems to pose for himself—and for us.

The actions and outcome of the lovers in *A Midsummer Night's Dream* may be instructive here, especially if we consider what enables the four young people finally to sort themselves out and unite in the promise of happy wedlock. The play begins with an ominous threat against one of the couples—Egeus's insistence that Hermia marry Demetrius, the young man of his choice, not hers. Therefore, Lysander and she flee Athens, but they get lost in the woods. During the night they encounter the other couple, the scorned Helena and the man she loves, Demetrius. In the ensuing confusions, Oberon's orders miscarry, thanks to Puck, but everything comes right in the end when Oberon sees to it that the magic potion is placed where it belongs and removed from where it does not. In this way, Oberon acts as the providence in the play, at least in this part of the action. By contrast, in the farcically performed but nonetheless significant play-within-the-play, "Pyramus and Thisbe," which the rude mechanicals perform in the last act, no providence intervenes to assist the lovers. They, like Romeo and Juliet (whose tragedy Shakespeare may here be parodying), die at the end, victims of misfortune or mischance.

Susan Snyder comes to a similar conclusion about the relation of comedy and tragedy in her excellent study *The Comic Matrix of Shakespeare's Tragedies.* Summing up her discussion of *Romeo and Juliet,* she says:

> Shakespeare's comic forms and conventions assume, first, the value of engagement with a mate, and second, the cooperation of forces beyond man, nat-

ural and otherwise, in achieving this mating and forestalling the consequences
of human irrationality and malice, as well as plain bad luck.

She then continues:

> To the extent that Shakespeare allowed bad luck to defeat love in *Romeo and
> Juliet,* we may see him as questioning the comic assumptions in that play, but
> the questioning does not go very deep. The lovers' relationship is presented as
> natural and right in itself. If it makes them irrationally impetuous, it is never-
> theless not this rashness that precipitates the tragedy.[1]

About *Romeo and Juliet* and the precipitating cause of the young lovers' tragedy,
critics have disagreed and doubtless will continue to do so. Romeo and Juliet are,
without question, rash and impetuous. Clearly that is true of Romeo, however less
certainly the statement may apply to Juliet.[2] Is this the main cause of their tragedy?
Or is it the feud that forces them to keep silent about their union? Or is it the absence of some benevolent providence, such as Romeo invokes when he has presentiments of disaster?[3] And if the cause is the absence of providence, why is it absent?
What is it that brings some to a comic, that is, a happy, resolution of their loves, and
others to a tragic, or unhappy, conclusion? Or is the ending of *Romeo and Juliet* as
unhappy as it may appear? Do these young lovers transcend their fate, achieving in
death what might have been impossible had they lived, given the intensity of their
feelings and the nature of their circumstances? By dying, do they blunt the slings
and arrows of their outrageous fortune, or simply fall victim to them?

These are only some of the questions that the play raises. Others will occur to
the careful and inquiring reader or spectator. For we should always remember that
Shakespeare wrote his plays for performance, not for publication, and certainly
not for modern textbooks and editions, useful as many of them are. He was first
and foremost a man of the theater, and it is in the theater—whether the Globe, a
modern playhouse, or the theater of the mind—that his plays take on life. And like
any man of the theater, Shakespeare knew that the script he prepared would probably have to be revised and adapted, possibly cut or added to, for stage presenta-
tion. A comparison of the two main texts—the first quarto published in 1597 and
the second one published in 1599—reveals the difference between the literary
manuscript, itself carrying evidence of revision during or soon after composition,
and an acting version of *Romeo and Juliet.* These differences and the theories relating to them are the basis for the discussion of the textual history of the play
below (Chapter 2). The discussion continues in Chapter 8 on performance, which
treats the stage history and offers some extracts of performance criticism. It may
come as a surprise to some that Shakespeare's play has not always appeared in the
form that either Quarto 1 or Quarto 2 presents but has undergone many other alterations and adaptations. It has even been updated and transposed to locations
other than Verona, Italy, as in the most recent film version by Baz Luhrmann. The
rationale for these alterations is also treated in the chapter on performance.

Finally, although this book deals mainly with traditional scholarly and critical methods of analyzing and understanding *Romeo and Juliet,* including source study as well as close reading and the analysis of Shakespeare's use of the arts of language, other approaches are described and illustrated. These include psychoanalytical criticism, feminist and gender criticism, myth and archetypal criticism. These highly specialized approaches require information and techniques that are becoming increasingly available and productive; accordingly, they merit further investigation. On the other hand, I have not found some other contemporary critical modes, such as cultural materialism or the New Historicism, quite as pertinent to the study of this play and have therefore not included them here. The Selected Bibliography at the end is far from exhaustive, but it includes items that may prove useful to anyone who wants to experience *Romeo and Juliet* as completely as possible.

This book is intended mainly as a reference tool for those wishing to study *Romeo and Juliet* in depth. The various chapters focus on major subjects that have occupied scholars and critics for many years. They begin, quite naturally, with a discussion of the textual history, which is basic to an understanding of any text—poem, play, or novel—for critics must know what they are dealing with before they begin analysis and interpretation. Sources are another important part of scholarly inquiry; they not only shed light on what Shakespeare is doing—and why—but at the same time, comparison of the sources and the play illuminates Shakespeare's creative processes. The chapters that follow deal directly with critical interpretation and understanding of the dramatic structure, characters, language, and themes found in *Romeo and Juliet.* These represent the most commonly used methods of approach, but Chapter 7 treats other possible approaches to understanding Shakespeare's tragedy. Last but by no means least, the stage history of the play forms the substance of the final chapter. Selective though it necessarily is, it provides an overview of performances on both stage and screen up to the present time.

All references to *Romeo and Juliet* are from the edition by G. B. Evans in the *New Cambridge Shakespeare.* References to other plays are from the *Riverside Shakespeare,* also edited by G. B. Evans.

I am grateful to the University of Delaware for granting me a sabbatical leave, during the course of which most of this book was written. I am once again greatly indebted to the Folger Shakespeare Library, whose resources I used daily during that sabbatical leave, which I spent in residence in Washington, D.C. Jill Levenson generously made available to me the text and commentary of her forthcoming Oxford edition of the play. In addition, she read several of my chapters in manuscript form and made a number of very useful comments and suggestions. For all of these favors, I thank her most heartily. Elise Goodman read the entire manuscript and helped with the proofreading. The dedication acknowledges only part of the debt I owe to her interest and encouragement. Finally, I extend gratitude to George F. Butler, acquisitions editor at Greenwood Press, for asking me to write this book, and to Norine Mudrick for overseeing its production.

NOTES

1. Susan Snyder, *The Comic Matrix of Shakespeare's Tragedies* (Princeton, N.J.: Princeton University Press, 1979), p. 73.

2. From the first she expresses doubts about the suddenness of their love (2.2.117–20), even though she pursues it as vigorously as Romeo.

3. Even before he lays eyes on Juliet, he appeals to Him that has the "steerage" of his course to direct his sail (1.4.112–13).

Romeo and Juliet

1

TEXTUAL HISTORY

THE EARLIEST TEXTS

Romeo and Juliet was first published in 1597 in quarto with the following statement on its title page: "An excellent conceited Tragedie of Romeo and Iuliet. As it hath been often (with great applause) plaid publiquely, by the right Honourable the L. of Hunsdon his Seruants. London, Printed by Iohn Danter." A second and much longer version appeared in quarto two years later, declaring on its title page that it is "*Newly corrected, augmented, and amended:* As it hath bene sundry times publiquely acted, by the right Honourable the Lord Chamberlaine his Seruants." It was printed by Thomas Creede and published by Cuthbert Burby.[1]

Much discussion has focused upon the provenance of the first quarto (Q1), comparing it with the second quarto (Q2), which most scholars believe is the more authentic one, printed from Shakespeare's own manuscript. Indeed, Q2 shows many signs of its being an authorial manuscript, such as the names of actors instead of characters in speech headings[2] and several passages in which both Shakespeare's first and second "shots"—that is, his original and then revised versions of lines—appear.[3] For a long time textual scholars believed that Q1 represents a pirated version of the play reconstructed from memory by a couple of actors, those playing the parts of Romeo and Paris.[4] More recently, the theory of memorial reconstruction has been challenged.[5] Whatever its origins, Q1 *Romeo* is clearly an acting version of the play,[6] tailored for the stage by someone, probably Shakespeare and/or some member of his company, who knew the play well and made revisions, some of them very minor ones, as he went along.

Comparison of the two texts is instructive. Then as now, apparently, a play presented to an acting company required certain adjustments before it was performed. Apart from various errors, such as ambiguous or erroneous speech headings requiring correction, Shakespeare's manuscript of *Romeo and Juliet* was probably too long (some 3,052 lines compared to Q1's 2,220).[7] If Alfred Hart is correct[8] in

A N EXCELLENT

conceited Tragedie

O F

Romeo and Iuliet.

As it hath been often (with great applaufe)
plaid publiquely, by the right Honourable the L. of *Hunfdon*
his Seruants.

LONDON,
Printed by Iohn Danter.
1 5 9 7.

Title page of the first quarto of *Romeo and Juliet* (1597).

THE
MOST EX=
cellent and lamentable
Tragedie, of Romeo
and *Iuliet*.

Newly corrected, augmented, and
amended:

As it hath bene sundry times publiquely acted, by the
right Honourable the Lord Chamberlaine
his Seruants.

LONDON
Printed by Thomas Creede, for Cuthbert Burby, and are to
be sold at his shop neare the Exchange.
1 5 9 9.

Title page of the second quarto of *Romeo and Juliet* (1599).

stating that the opening Chorus of *Romeo and Juliet* gives the approximate length of an Elizabethan play ("the two-hours' traffic of our stage"), then some serious cutting must have seemed necessary before the play was acted.[9] Some of it could be done before rehearsals began, other cuts made during rehearsals, and still others after initial performances, as current stage practice also indicates. For example, Juliet's speech beginning 2.5 is drastically curtailed. In Q2 it reads:

> *Iu.* The clocke strooke nine when I did send the Nurse,
> In halfe an houre she promised to returne,
> Perchance she cannot meete him, thats not so:
> Oh she is lame, loues heraulds should be thoughts,
> Which ten times faster glides then the Suns beames,   5
> Driuing backe shadowes ouer lowring hills.
> Therefore do nimble piniond doues draw loue,
> And therefore hath the wind swift *Cupid* wings:
> Now is the Sun vpon the highmost hill,
> Of this dayes iourney, and from nine till twelue,   10
> Is three long houres, yet she is not come,
> Had she affections and warme youthfull bloud,
> She would be as swift in motion as a ball,
> My words would bandie her to my sweete loue.
>   *M.* And his to me, but old folks, many fain as they wer dead,
> Vnwieldie, slowe, heauie, and pale as lead.   16
>   *Enter Nurse.*
> O God she comes, ô hony Nurse what newes?
> Has thou met with him? send thy man away.

In Q1 it appears much curtailed:

> *Iul.* The clocke stroke nine when I did send **my** Nursse
> In halfe an houre she promist to returne.
> **Perhaps** she cannot **finde** him. Thats not so.
> Oh she is **lazie,** Loues heralds should be thoughts,
> **And moue more swift, than hastie powder fierd,**
> **Doth hurrie from the fearfull Cannons mouth.**
>   *Enter Nurse.*
> O **now** she comes. **Tell me gentle** Nurse,
> **What sayes my Loue?**

The bold words in the Q1 passage show local variants—examples of verbal "tinkerings" characteristic of authorial revision, rather than simple stage abridgment—but of greater significance is the nature of the cuts.[10] The adapter clearly felt that the extended conceit (ll. 4–8) was inessential and substituted instead a briefer metaphor for it, possibly suggested by the cannonball mentioned in line 13.

Similarly, at the opening of 3.2, Juliet's soliloquy goes on for thirty-five lines. In Q1, the speech is reduced to just the first four lines until the Nurse's entrance. A lot of very beautiful verse is thus sacrificed for dramatic expediency. By eliminating the lyrical passages, the adapter tightened the dramatic structure of the play so that the action moved forward at a quicker pace. But not only were Juliet's flights of fancy curtailed in this way. Many other cuts were necessary to bring the playscript to a desirable length and keep the action moving. From the very opening scene onward, Q1 skillfully adapts what Shakespeare originally wrote to a swifter paced drama that loses little of its *dramatic* impact, whatever losses it may sustain in its poetry.

The reviser had more on his mind, however, than just cutting the text. He also attempted to clarify some passages as well as the action. Interestingly, although it contributes absolutely nothing to the dramatic action, he retained all of Mercutio's Queen Mab speech (1.4.55–95). Shakespeare was evidently much concerned with this speech, which has since become one of the most famous in the play. From the signs of revision apparent in Q2, he labored a good deal over this passage and went on to revise it further in Q1, causing the printer in both quartos considerable difficulty in setting the lines. Hence, in Q2 most of the lines are printed as prose, and in Q1 some lines are missing. Here is the speech as it appears in Q1, with local variants (again, likely indications of authorial tinkering) highlighted in bold type, the Q2 reading following in brackets:

> She is the fairies Midwife and **doth** come
> in shape no bigger than an Agat stone
> On the forefinger of **a Burgermaster** [Q2 an Alderman],
> Drawne with a teeme of little Atomi   57
> **A thwart** [Q2 ouer] mens noses **when** they lie a sleepe.
> Her waggon spokes **are** made of [Q2 long] spinners **webs** [Q2 legs],
> The couer, of the wings of Grashoppers,
> **The** traces **are the Moon shine watrie beames,**   63
> [Q2: her traces of the smallest spider web, her collors of the moonshines
>   watry beams,]
> **The collors** [Q2 her whip of] crickets bones, the lash of filmes [Q2
>   Philome],
> Her waggoner **is** a small gray coated **flie** [Q2 Gnat]
> Not halfe so big as **is** a [Q2 round] little worme,   68
> **Pickt** [Q2 prickt] from the lasie finger of a **maide** [Q2 man; Q2 then has
>   three lines not in Q1][11]
> And in this **sort** [Q2 state] she gallops **vp and downe** [Q2 night by night]
> Through Louers braines, and then they dream of loue:
> **O're** [Q2 On] Courtiers knees: **who** [Q2 that] strait on cursies dreame   72
> [Q2 adds: ore Lawyers fingers who strait dreame on fees]
> O're Ladies lips, who dreame on kisses strait:
> Which oft the angrie Mab with blisters plagues,
> Because their breath**es** with sweet meats tainted are:

Sometimes she gallops ore a **Lawers lap** [Q2 Courtiers nose]   77
And then dreames he of smelling out a sute,
And sometime comes she with a tithe pigs taile,
Tickling a Parsons nose **that** [Q2 as a] lies asleepe,
And then dreames he of another benefice: 81
Sometime she **gallops** [Q2 driueth] ore a souldiers **nose** [Q2 neck]
And then dreames he of cutting forraine throats,
Of breaches ambuscadoes, **countermines**, [Q2 spanish blades]
Of healthes fiue fadome deepe, and then anon   85
Drums in his eare: at which he startes and wakes,
And [Q2 adds: being thus frighted,] sweares a Praier or two and sleeps
    againe.

The last several lines of the Queen Mab speech reveal some interesting textual
problems. Q1 alters the sequence of Q2, continuing the imagery of sleepers, which
Q2 interrupts. In the process Q1 loses a line and a half of regular iambic pentame-
ters, its own versification becoming irregular, as if the revision had not yet been
put into final form. Actually, this is a characteristic found elsewhere in Q1, one
often attributed to the faulty memory of a reporter rather than to revision. But as
we have seen, Q2 gives abundant evidence of Shakespeare's revising hand.

Q1:   This is that Mab **that makes** maids lie on their backes,   92
        And **proues** them women of good cariage: (the night,
        This is **the** verie Mab that plats the manes of Horses in
        And **plats** the Elfelocks in foule sluttish haire,   90
        Which once vntangled much misfortune **breedes**.   91

Q2:   this is that very Mab that plats the manes of horses in
        the night: and bakes the Elklocks in foule sluttish
        haires, which once vntangled, much misfortune bodes.   91
        This is the hag, when maides lie on their backs,
        That presses them and learnes them first to beare,
        Making them women of good carriage:
        This is she.   95

Further evidence of Shakespeare's revision of Q2 occurs at 3.3.37–44. Romeo
refers to flies who light on Juliet's hand

Q2:   And steale immortal blessing from her lips,   37
        Who euen in pure and vestall modestie
        Still blush, as thinking their owne kisses sin.
        This may flyes do, when I from this, must flie   40
        And sayest thou yet, that exile is not death?
        But *Romeo* may not, he is banished.
        Flies may do this, but I from this must flie: 43
        They are freemen, but I am banished.

Recognizing the revision here, modern editors place lines 42–44 after line 39 and delete line 40.[12] But might not the author or the adapter have had still another, third "shot"? Q1 deletes 38–41 and 44, and revises the following lines, expanding and clarifying the sense:

> Q2:   Hadst thou no poyson mixt, no sharpe ground knife,
>   No sudden meane of death, though nere so meane,
>   But banished to kill me: Banished?
>   O Frier, the damned vse that word in hell:

> Q1:   Oh Father hadst thou no strong poyson mixt,
>   No sharpe ground knife, no present meane of death,
>   Though nere so meane, but banishment[13]
>   To torture me withall: ah, banished.
>   O Frier, the damned vse that word in hell:

If Shakespeare continued to revise his play, as seems likely, then a conceivable sequence of events is this: he first wrote out a full draft of his play, revising some parts as he went along. Since the draft was too lengthy for playhouse performance, a shorter draft was made, with further revisions as well as cuts, including numerous tinkerings with individual words or phrases. This became the acting version of the play, from which the promptbook was prepared. This revised, second draft was then printed in 1597 in the first quarto. Two years later, Burby published the second quarto, its title page proclaiming that this text was "*Newly corrected, augmented, and amended,*" but only "*augmented*" reflects actual fact with anything like complete accuracy. Much later, in 1609, Q2 was reprinted, and from this third quarto the Folio text was set up without any significant alteration and published with the rest of Shakespeare's collected plays in 1623.[14]

If this theory of the provenance of the two basic texts (Q1 and Q2) is correct, two further problems remain that perhaps may never be solved. The first concerns how Danter obtained a copy of the playscript, which he was unable in any case to completely set up in type (he was found to be printing an unauthorized book, and, as a consequence, his two presses were "defaced and made unserviceable for prynting").[15] As Peter Blayney has shown, so-called pirated plays had hardly any commercial value, since, given the costs of production and the income they could generate—given, too, the risks that might be involved—there was little incentive to publish them.[16] But however Danter came by his copy, and whatever may have motivated him to publish it, one scene in particular—2.6—has raised serious textual questions. In Q1 this scene seems to have been composed by another hand entirely, it is so different from the style elsewhere in the play. Various theories have been proposed, among them that Danter asked his friend Henry Chettle, a contemporary playwright, to furnish the scene that may have been damaged beyond repair in Danter's copy.[17] Whether Chettle or someone else composed the scene, it seems clear that Shakespeare did not.[18]

Recently, Donald W. Foster has proposed an alternative theory regarding the two texts.[19] Using an elaborate computer program he developed called SHAXICON, which is based primarily upon Shakespeare's rare word usage, Foster argues that Q1 preceded Q2 in composition, that yet another manuscript, from which Q1 derives, was once extant and on which cuts and revisions were made. Shakespeare later revised and augmented this version to produce the manuscript that then superseded the Q1 version on the stage and from which Q2 was printed. He also dates the play earlier than 1596, to about 1593/1594. The important question that Foster does not answer or even raise is why Shakespeare would further revise and considerably lengthen his play—something that goes against usual theatrical practice. On the other hand, I believe Foster is right in rejecting memorial reconstruction as behind Q1 and in accepting Shakespeare's responsibility for both versions of his play.[20]

MODERN EDITIONS

The second quarto was reprinted in the third quarto of 1609, which in its turn provided the copy for the text that appeared in the First Folio (1623), the first collected edition of Shakespeare's plays compiled by his fellow actors and shareholders, John Heminges and Henry Condell. All other subsequent editions of the Folio, as well as the quartos printed in 1622 and 1637, thus derive from Q2,[21] none bearing any authorial correction or amendment, but all capable of introducing new errors or correcting old ones.

Modern editing of *Romeo and Juliet* began with Nicholas Rowe's edition in 1709, based on the text printed in the Fourth Folio (1685). Alexander Pope's edition (1723–1725) first took note of the quartos and began the process of eclectic editing that continued through the eighteenth and the nineteenth century and in most editions ever since. That is, modern editors have presumed to correct the text of Q2 by using as the basis for their emendations variant readings found in Q1 or any of the editions subsequent to Q2, including many of the great eighteenth-century editors after Alexander Pope, such as Lewis Theobald, Edward Capell, Samuel Johnson, and Edmond Malone. Many of the stage directions in modern editions, for example, derive from Q1, and some of the corrected textual readings derive from that quarto or the work of eighteenth-century and later editors. Modern editors have also corrected mislineation of verse and verse printed as prose or vice versa.

Fully annotated editions, such as the *New Variorum Shakespeare* edited by H. H. Furness (1871) or, more recently, the New Arden edition by Brian Gibbons (1980) and the *New Cambridge Shakespeare* edition by G. B. Evans (1984), provide collations of the most important textual variants found in earlier editions. These are found immediately below the text in smaller type. In editions of Shakespeare's complete works, such as the *Riverside Shakespeare* and David Bevington's *Complete Works of Shakespeare*, the collations are found at the end of the play. These tend to record chiefly the departures from the editor's control text, rather than anything like a historical collation such as that found in fully annotated, single-text editions.

Among the best current single-text editions of *Romeo and Juliet* is the New Arden edition, which includes lengthy abstracts from Arthur Brooke's *Romeus and Juliet* in an appendix, as well as an introduction that covers analyses of the textual history, sources, stage history, and interpretation of the play. Detailed commentary appears on the same page of the text below the selective historical collations. The *New Cambridge Shakespeare* likewise has lengthy extracts from Brooke's poem in an appendix, a full introduction, and commentary below the collations, which are fuller than the New Arden's, heavily burdened as they are with extensive readings from Q1. Jill Levenson's forthcoming Oxford edition will include, besides the introduction, collations, and commentary as in the preceding editions, a complete modernized text of Q1. George Walton Williams's critical edition of *Romeo and Juliet* (1964) is the only recent original-spelling edition. Its collations, which appear at the end of the volume, are based on the early quartos; footnotes to the text record rejected Q2 readings as emended in subsequent editions. Appended to the volume are extensive textual notes, staging notes, a list of press variants collated from copies of Q2, and a list of emendations of accidentals (i.e., nonsubstantive spelling and punctuation variants). These editions are especially useful for advanced undergraduate and graduate courses.

Complete editions of Shakespeare's works, such as the *Riverside Shakespeare*, Bevington's, and the Norton, typically include critical introductions to the play that give briefer analyses of the textual history, sources, and stage history than single-text editions. The emphasis of the introductions tends to be on interpretations of the play, sometimes written by a critic other than the textual editor. All of these include commentary and glosses on the same page as the text. The Oxford *Complete Works* (1988) is an exception, providing only a carefully edited text, a two-page introduction, and a glossary at the end of the volume, but no notes of any kind.[22] Its companion volume, *A Textual Companion*, provides a full textual introduction, collations, and discussion of emendations and rejected readings. All of these editions are based on Q2 and regard Q1 as a memorially reconstructed text based upon an acting version of the play.

A number of inexpensive paperback editions are also available besides the softcover copies of the *New Cambridge Shakespeare* and the New Arden and Oxford (World Classics) editions. These include those in the Signet, Folger, Pelican, Everyman, and Bantam series. The Folger *Romeo and Juliet* has recently been reedited by Barbara Mowat and Paul Werstine. The Signet includes a selection of several critical essays at the end of the volume. The Bantam reprints Bevington's edition in his complete Shakespeare. All of these contain critical introductions and gloss difficult words and phrases at the bottom of the page, except for the Folger, which has notes on pages facing the text, as does the Everyman, edited by John Andrews. As auxiliary texts in survey courses or other undergraduate or high school courses that include only one or two plays, these editions are very serviceable.

NOTES

1. Three other quartos were printed in the early seventeenth century: Q3 (1609), Q4 (1622), and Q5 (1637), all for John Smethwick. The copy for the First Folio (1623) was Q3. None of these are substantive or authoritative editions, being mainly reprints of previous editions.

2. See W. W. Greg, *The Shakespeare First Folio* (Oxford: Clarendon Press, 1955), p. 229.

3. Friar Lawrence's opening lines in 2.3 repeat in slightly different form four of the last lines of Romeo's speech in 2.2. Many editors take Romeo's lines as Shakespeare's first shot, and Friar Lawrence's as the revised version. Similarly, at 5.3.108–15, another duplication of lines appears. The printer evidently failed to notice which lines were canceled and printed both sets. For other examples of revision in Q2, see Grace Ioppolo, *Revising Shakespeare* (Cambridge, Mass.: Harvard University Press, 1991), pp. 90–91.

4. The most extensive analysis based upon this theory is Harry Hoppe, *The Bad Quarto of "Romeo and Juliet"* (Ithaca, N.Y.: Cornell University Press, 1948). See also Kathleen Irace, *Reforming the "Bad" Quartos* (Newark: University of Delaware Press, 1994), pp. 126–31, who suggests that the actor playing Paris may also have doubled in the role of Mercutio.

5. See, for example, David Farley-Hills, "The 'Bad' Quarto of *Romeo and Juliet*," *Shakespeare Survey* 49 (1996): 27–44; Laurie Maguire, *Shakespearean Suspect Texts* (Cambridge: Cambridge University Press, 1996), pp. 301–2; and Jay L. Halio, "Handy-Dandy: Q1/Q2 *Romeo and Juliet*," in *Shakespeare's "Romeo and Juliet": Texts, Contexts, and Interpretation*, ed. Jay L. Halio (Newark: University of Delaware Press, 1995), pp. 123–50.

6. Cp. Farley-Hills, "The 'Bad' Quarto," p. 28.

7. See George Walton Williams's critical old-spelling edition (Durham, NC: Duke University Press, 1964), p. xii.

8. Hart maintains that the average length of Elizabethan plays (excluding Shakespeare's and Ben Jonson's) was 2,500 lines long. See *Shakespeare and the Homilies* (1934; rpt. New York: Octagon, 1970), pp. 77–153. In "Back to Basics: Thinking about the *Hamlet* First Quarto," in *The "Hamlet" First Published*, ed. Thomas Clayton (Newark: University of Delaware Press, 1992), pp. 266–70, Steven Urkowitz questions Hart's use of an "average" figure and argues that the length of Elizabethan plays varied. But using Hart's data, Urkowitz notes that a large group of plays were about 2,000 lines long, another large group 2,600–3,000 lines long, and the rest from 1,600 to 3,200 lines. Q2 *Romeo and Juliet* would therefore be near the upper limit, whereas Q1 would be closer to the typical playhouse length.

9. See Random Cloud [Randall McLeod], "The Marriage of Good and Bad Quartos," *Shakespeare Quarterly* 33 (1982): 421–31, esp. p. 426. Recently, Paul Werstine has challenged the received opinion that the "bad quartos" represent shortened versions of plays for acting companies' provincial tours; see "Touring and the Construction of Shakespeare Textual Criticism," in *Textual Formations and Reformations*, ed. Laurie Maguire and Thomas L. Berger (Newark: University of Delaware Press, 1998).

10. For authorial revision of this sort, see John Kerrigan, "Revision, Adaptation, and the Fool in *King Lear*," in *The Division of the Kingdoms: Shakespeare's Two Versions of "King Lear*," ed. Gary Taylor and Michael Warren (Oxford: Clarendon Press, 1983), pp. 195–245.

11. The lines are: "Her Charriot is an emptie Hasel nut, Made by the Ioyner squirrel or old Grub, time out amind, the Fairies Coatchmakers:" Modern editors usually place these lines after 58, as more appropriate in that context. See, for example, Brian Gibbons's note on 1.4.59–61 in his New Arden edition (London: Methuen, 1980) and Williams's note in his edition, p. 110.

12. See, for example, Gibbons's textual note in his New Arden edition, pp. 176–77; Williams's note in his edition, pp. 128–29; and the supplementary note in the *New Cambridge Shakespeare*, ed. G. B. Evans (Cambridge: Cambridge University Press, 1984), p. 202. Cp. E. Pearlman, "Shakespeare at Work," *English Literary Renaissance* 24 (1994): 319–21, who discusses "Shakespeare's effort to refine his conceits" in this "rhetorically complex passage."

13. Q1 again alters "banished" to "Banishment" at the end of Romeo's speech (l. 50).

14. Greg, *Shakespeare First Folio*, pp. 231–32.

15. Ibid., p. 225.

16. Farley–Hills speculates that Q1 may have been published as a "money-spinner and trailer for Q2 by arrangement with Shakespeare's company" ("The 'Bad' Quarto," p. 42). See also Peter W. M. Blayney, "The Publication of Playbooks," in *A New History of English Drama*, ed. John D. Cox and David Scott Kastan (New York: Columbia University Press, 1997), pp. 383–422, esp. pp. 405–16.

17. Sidney Thomas, "Henry Chettle and the First Quarto of *Romeo and Juliet*," *Review of English Studies*, n.s., 1 (1950): 8–16.

18. Cp. Farley-Hills, "The 'Bad' Quarto," p. 35, who believes either that the redactor (who was not Shakespeare) wrote 2.6 when the page on which Shakespeare's original was found missing or that Shakespeare rewrote it after Q1 was published.

19. Donald W. Foster, "The Webbing of *Romeo and Juliet*," in *Critical Essays on "Romeo and Juliet,"* ed. Joseph A. Porter (New York: G. K. Hall, 1997), pp. 131–49.

20. Ibid., p. 133. Grace Iopplo also considers the possibility that Shakespeare revised his play after Q1 was, as she says, "reported and printed" (see *Revising Shakespeare*, p. 93). Farley-Hills pursues this suggestion in his essay, though he does not accept the idea of a reported text for Q1 and argues that a redactor other than Shakespeare was responsible for the Q1 version that was prepared for touring in the provinces ("The 'Bad' Quarto," p. 34).

21. Q4 (1622) shows some signs of Q1 influence, the printers apparently having consulted a copy of that edition. Q5 (1637) was reprinted from Q4.

22. The editor for *Romeo and Juliet* was John Jowett, who also wrote the section on the play in the *Textual Companion*. The Oxford text is the basis for the Norton edition, which essentially reprints all of the texts in the Oxford *Complete Works* and supplies commentary and notes as well as new, lengthier introductions.

2

CONTEXTS AND SOURCES

Shakespeare's *Romeo and Juliet* (1595–1596) falls within what is sometimes referred to as his "lyrical" period, the group of plays that includes *Richard II*, *A Midsummer Night's Dream*, and at least the last act of *The Merchant of Venice*. In these plays, Shakespeare indulges in flights of lyricism, such as Richard II's soliloquy (5.5.1–66), Theseus's discourse on the imagination (5.1.4–22), or Juliet's soliloquy at the beginning of 3.2. The lyricism occurs at the expense of dramatic action, which seems to mark time as the poet indulges the expression of emotion, attitude, or feeling for its own apparent sake. The poetry is unquestionably beautiful and moving, as Shakespeare elaborates one metaphor or poetic conceit after another. To be sure, in his later plays, Shakespeare learned to fuse poetry and dramatic action more completely. Compare, for example, Juliet's invocation to night (3.2.17–25) with Lady Macbeth's (1.5.37–53) and notice how more tightly structured the latter is both in its poetic texture and in its ability to generate dramatic tension. Nevertheless, this early romantic tragedy by Shakespeare has remained a perennial favorite in our time, as it was during the seventeenth century, when it seems Oxford undergraduates turned to it far more often than any of Shakespeare's plays.

Other comparisons, not only to Shakespeare's earlier and later work, but to his use of his source materials, are also useful and demonstrate to a considerable extent how his creative process functioned. While scholars have noticed possible debts to authors who previously wrote about Romeo and Juliet—Luigi da Porto, Luigi Groto, Matteo Bandello, Pierre Boaistuau, and William Painter—Shakespeare's main source for his play was Arthur Brooke's long narrative poem *The Tragicall Historye of Romeus and Juliet*.[1] Based on Bandello's version (in Boiastuau's French translation), Brooke's poem was written in poulter's measure (or fourteeners) and first published in 1562. It was later reprinted in 1582 and 1587, evidencing the story's popularity during Elizabeth's reign. Although at the end of his address "To the Reader" Brooke mentions having seen "the same argument lately set foorth on stage" (p. 285),[2] no English drama on the subject before Shakespeare's is otherwise known to have existed.

In his prefatory remarks, Brooke says that the purpose of his tale is to describe for the reader "a coople of unfortunate lovers, thralling themselves to unhonest desire, neglecting the authoritie and advise of parents and frendes, conferring their principall counsels with dronken gossyppes, and superstitious friers (the naturally fitte instruments of unchastitie) attemptyng all adventures of peryll, for thattaynyng of their wished lust" and so forth (p. 284). But however unsympathetic or Puritanical Brooke's Protestant attitude appears toward the unhappy fate of the two young lovers in his preface, and however moralistic it is, the poem itself, like Shakespeare's play, actually generates a good deal of sympathy for the couple.

Brooke begins his poem with a description of Verona and the long-standing feud between the Capulets and the Montagues, which Prince Escalus has been trying to end with little success. What Brooke describes, Shakespeare vigorously dramatizes in his opening scene, showing with powerful effect the enmity that has grown up between the two noble houses and the terrible strife it causes. A fight scene much later in Brooke's poem (ll. 993–1007) may have suggested the conflict Shakespeare uses to begin with, which ends with Prince Escalus's warning against further civil strife. Shakespeare's portrait of lovesick Romeo derives from Brooke, who includes advice from a friend to Romeus that he should abandon his unrequited love and look elsewhere. Accordingly, Romeus and five others attend a masked ball at Christmas given by the Capulets, during which Romeus sees Juliet and falls in love with her, quite forgetting his earlier love (ll. 197–228).

Brooke describes the passion Romeus feels for Juliet as a "poyson" that swiftly spreads throughout his bones and veins (l. 221), and in an editorial comment earlier (ll. 151–54) remarks that Romeus would have been better off after all not to heed his friend's earlier advice. Except for the remarks in the Prologue and Romeo's presentiments of disaster (1.4.106–12), Shakespeare does not prejudge the action, which in any event was well enough known to many of the literate members in his audience. Rather, he lets it unfold, embellishing it dramatically and lyrically with episodes and speeches that have no precedent in Brooke's poem.

A major addition is the development of Mercutio's character. In *Romeus and Juliet,* Mercutio is mentioned only as one of the dancers who sits on one side of Juliet when Romeus sits on the other at the ball:

> A courtier that eche where was highly had in pryce,
> For he was coorteous of his speche, and pleasant of devise
> Even as a Lyon would emong the lambes be bolde,
> Such was emong the bashfull maydes, Mercutio to beholde. (ll. 255–58)

The only other detail Brooke adds (borrowing from Bandello) is that Mercutio has extremely cold hands, which, accordingly, Juliet drops to hold Romeus's warmer one. From this briefest of sketches, Shakespeare builds a much fuller portrait of Mercutio as Romeo's close friend, a neurotic (as aptly played by John McEnery in the Franco Zeffirelli film) who tells of Queen Mab and her behavior (1.4.54–94, another Shakespearean invention), disconcerting Romeo as he does so. Later, he plays a principal part in the fight that results not only in his death, but in Tybalt's also and Romeo's banishment. Mercutio's ironic wit plays off against Romeo's romantic attitude, becoming a foil to it. When he dies, the play turns from its comic potential into tragedy.

While Shakespeare expands the role of Mercutio and his important action in the play, he condenses and dramatically heightens the courtship and marriage of Romeo and Juliet. Although Romeus and Juliet fall in love at first sight just as Shakespeare's lovers do, what takes place over a period of weeks before the wedding and then months before Romeo's banishment in Brooke's poem occurs in a matter of days in Shakespeare's play. In this way, Shakespeare emphasizes the impetuousness of the young lovers and their passionate love for each other, who marry and consummate their love within a span of forty-eight hours.[3] The Nurse appears much earlier in Shakespeare than in Brooke, and her character is amplified for both comic and dramatic effect, but she serves the essential function in each work as a go-between for Juliet and Romeo. Friar Lawrence's role is also essentially the same. He not only agrees to marry the young lovers so as to prevent them from falling into sinful intercourse, but he also hopes that the marriage may help to heal the feud between their families (ll. 607–10), a point that Shakespeare, too, makes explicit (2.3.91–92).

In Brooke's poem, Fortune plays a large part. Her fickle nature is often invoked or referred to by various characters as well as by the author in his editorial comments, like those he makes immediately after Romeus and Juliet begin enjoying their conjugal existence and just before the family feuding breaks out again (ll. 902–14). It is during this fray, which Romeus's efforts prove futile to stop, that Tybalt, who hates all Montagues, spots Romeus. He draws on him, forcing him to defend himself, not heeding Romeus's appeals for aid in stopping the slaughter. The blows Tybalt directs at Romeus enrage him, and he finally slays his opponent. Afterward, as punishment Romeus is banished, though not before he has a last night with Juliet.

Juliet, like Romeus, is at first frantic at the news that he and she must be parted. But just as Friar Lawrence had earlier calmed Romeus down, so Romeus now calms Juliet, rejecting her plea that she accompany him in disguise as his manservant. Under Friar Lawrence's advice, he will go to Mantua, try to win friends, and sue for a reprieve from Prince Escalus, using whatever influence he can obtain to do so. Then he will openly claim Juliet as his wife. Reluctantly, Juliet agrees, but after he leaves her in a scene that Shakespeare renders far more eloquent and moving than Brooke, Juliet continues grieving inconsolably.

Her mother, a shadowy figure up to now in Brooke's poem, worries that Juliet's grief is excessive, and when Juliet responds somewhat cryptically that her tears are no longer for Tybalt's death, Lady Capulet starts wondering what could be the matter. She determines it must be that Juliet wants to be married, since many of her friends are already married. She therefore goes to her husband and expresses her views. He agrees and sets about finding a suitable husband. It is only here that the County Paris enters the story in Brooke's poem, and only briefly—not as in Shakespeare, where at 1.3.75, Juliet's mother mentions Paris's suit, thus raising early with her daughter the issue of matrimony. The match is proposed, Juliet is forced to comply, and she seeks remedy for her anguish from Friar Lawrence, who gives her the potion that will put her in a brief deathlike trance. Meanwhile, Friar Lawrence says he will write to Romeus, letting him know of their plan and telling him to meet him at Juliet's tomb after the funeral to carry her off to Mantua.

Brooke's Juliet has fearful hallucinations just before she takes the potion, just as Shakespeare's Juliet does, though Shakespeare gives his Juliet much more vivid and detailed lines, thereby making her speech (4.3.14–58) more moving and her action more brave. Similarly, the scene between Romeo and the Apothecary in Shakespeare's play is more dramatic, the description of the Apothecary's shop more vivid and detailed than in Brooke's poem. But in both poem and play, Fortune, or Chance, here plays a crucial part insofar as Friar John is never able to deliver the letter Friar Lawrence has written to Romeus, because he is detained (in fact, quarantined) in a house infected by plague. Thus, when Romeus's man (called Peter in Brooke's poem) arrives with the news of Juliet's death, Romeus sets about planning to commit suicide beside her in her tomb.

Shakespeare complicates the final scene by introducing a grieving County Paris at the tomb, who gets there before Romeo. His grief compares with Romeo's and becomes its foil. When Paris challenges Romeo, Romeo does not recognize him until after he has killed him, adding further catastrophe to the tragedy. Again, in both Brooke's poem and Shakespeare's play, Chance plays a role, as Juliet's husband dies before she awakens. When Friar Lawrence arrives and enters the tomb with Peter, Juliet rejects his pleas to leave with him and enter a convent, preferring to die by her husband's side. The Watch, seeing a light in the tomb and suspecting grave robbers, arrive and later apprehend the Friar and Peter, who are brought before the Prince for judgment.

Brooke's Friar Lawrence has a very long speech, which begins with an *apologia pro vita sua* and some sermonizing on recent events. Shakespeare's Friar is much briefer, as befits the denouement of his play, simply recounting his actions. Brooke's poem ends with the Friar's acquittal (though he decides to become a hermit thereafter), Peter's acquittal, the Apothecary's sentence to be hanged, and the Nurse's banishment (for keeping Juliet's marriage secret from her parents). The Montagues and the Capulets are at last reconciled, and their children are placed together in a high marble tomb, beneath which are set "Great store of cunning Epitaphes, in honor of theyr death" (l. 3016), visible even to the present day. Shakespeare's ending postpones the specifics of the sentencing, Prince Escalus proclaiming instead, simply and profoundly, "All are punished" (5.3.295). Montague and Capulet, reconciled, declare that they will raise statues of Romeo and Juliet in "pure gold," "Poor sacrifices of our enmity" (5.3.299, 304), as Escalus announces the "glooming peace" that this morning brings.

Shakespeare drew on other sources besides Brooke for some aspects of his play. For example, the dueling episodes in act 3 are indebted to handbooks on dueling that some scholars identify as Vincent Saviolo's *Practice* (1595).[4] Brawling was severely frowned upon by the Tudor monarchs, as well as by the church. Henry VII, Henry VIII, and Elizabeth I all issued proclamations against fighting in public, but despite these measures, civil disorder repeatedly erupted in town and country throughout the sixteenth century. Violence broke out in Fleet Street and the Strand in London, and feuding disturbed the peace of whole counties.[5] Elizabeth's policies gradually took hold and reduced the amount of civil disturbance. Her efforts are reflected to some degree in the exhortations and threats of Prince Escalus, just as the scenes of conflict between the feuding houses in *Romeo and Juliet* reflect social conflict in her realm during Shakespeare's time. Nevertheless, dueling remained a contemporary preoccupation among Elizabethan gentlemen, who studied manuals such as Saviolo's and others' and learned how to fence.[6]

Other aspects of society pictured in *Romeo and Juliet* may or may not accurately reflect Elizabethan customs and mores. It is clear that the male head of the house might rule as a despot quite in the way Capulet rules his household and bestow his children in marriage as he saw fit.[7] It is by no means clear, however, that marriages among teenagers as young as Juliet and (presumably) Romeo commonly occurred. The historian Peter Laslett has argued persuasively that such a union as that between Romeo and Juliet was in fact exceptional, not typical.[8] The mean age for brides among the gentry in the early seventeenth century was about twenty-one or twenty-two; for bridegrooms, about twenty-six. It was slightly lower for members of the aristocracy (nineteen and twenty-four, respectively). Marriage at an age as young as fourteen was rare, though not unheard of.[9] More to the point is the age at which women might expect to bear children. Laslett argues that Lady Capulet's statement regarding the age at which she bore Juliet is extraordinary, since it is doubtful whether she or her daughter could be capable of sexual relations, let alone procreation, at age thirteen. But perhaps that is just it: Shakespeare was presenting exceptional people, as writers often do, rather than ordinary people.[10] In other respects, too, the behavior in *Romeo and Juliet* is extraordinary, as, for example, the clandestine marriage that Friar Lawrence agrees to conduct. Private marriages performed by someone in holy orders were not unheard of, but hardly commonplace.[11] The possibility of clandestine marriage, however, enabled underage unions to occur, or so it seems.[12]

To return to literary sources: Several cantos in Edmund Spenser's *Faerie Queene* probably inspired part of the fairy lore that Mercutio draws upon in his Queen Mab speech, although Thomas Nashe's *Terrors of the Night* (1594) may also have been an influence.[13] Without question, *Romeo and Juliet* draws on the sonnet tradition that flourished during the Continental Renaissance and arrived in the sixteenth century in England, where Sir Thomas Wyatt, the Earl of Surrey, Sir Philip Sidney, Spenser, and many others developed it. The movement reached its peak and began to decline at about the time Shakespeare composed his play, which

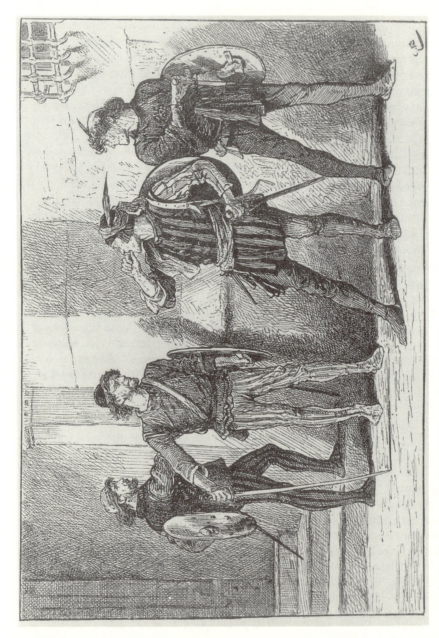

Illustration from the Henry Irving Shakespeare (1888), 1.1.44.

pokes fun at some of its excesses even as it capitalizes on this legacy.[14] Other literary works that may have left their mark on this play are Samuel Daniel's *Complaint of Rosamund* (1592) and John Eliot's *Ortho-epia Gallica* (1593).[15] Shakespeare was familiar with these works and others, such as Painter's version of the story (from which he may have borrowed Romeo's name instead of using Brooke's for his hero), but we err if we think of Shakespeare composing his play with an array of books open before him. Rather, his mind was like a sponge that gathered to itself much that he had read and heard and that supplied him, consciously or not, with images and ideas, phrases and analogues, that permeated his work,[16] usually in altered and superior—that is, more intensely poetic—form.

NOTES

1. See Geoffrey Bullough, ed., *Narrative and Dramatic Sources of Shakespeare,* 8 vols. (London: Routledge; New York: Columbia University Press, 1957–1975), vol. 1, pp. 269–74, and Kenneth Muir, *The Sources of Shakespeare's Plays* (New Haven, Conn.: Yale University Press, 1978), pp. 38–39. In "Romeo and Juliet before Shakespeare," *Studies in Philology* 81 (1984): 325–47, Jill Levenson traces the narrative tradition from da Porto to Brooke and finally to Shakespeare's innovative treatment of it.

2. All page and line references are to Bullough's reprinting in *Narrative and Dramatic Sources.*

3. Muir, *Sources,* p. 40.

4. See, for example, Jill Levenson, " '*Alla stoccado* carries it away': Codes of Violence in *Romeo and Juliet,*" in *Shakespeare's "Romeo and Juliet": Texts, Contexts, and Interpretation,* ed. Jay L. Halio (Newark: University of Delaware Press, 1995), pp. 83–96, and Joan Ozark Holmer, " 'Draw, if you be men': Saviolo's Significance for *Romeo and Juliet,*" *Shakespeare Quarterly* 45 (1994): 163–89. Donald W. Foster, however, disputes Holmer's claim for Saviolo's influence on the play and maintains that Shakespeare got his terminology from John Florio's *Second Frutes* (1591); see "The Webbing of *Romeo and Juliet,*" in *Critical Essays on "Romeo and Juliet,"* ed. Joseph A. Porter (New York: G. K. Hall, 1997), pp. 136–41.

5. Levenson, "Codes of Violence," p. 85, citing Charles Edelman, *Brawl Ridiculous: Swordfighting in Shakespeare's Plays* (Manchester: Manchester University Press, 1992), pp. 17, 174–75, and Lawrence Stone, *The Crisis of the Aristocracy, 1558–1641* (Oxford: Clarendon Press, 1965), pp. 229–32.

6. Levenson mentions Sir William Segar's *The Book of Honor and Arms* (1590) and Giacomo di Grassi's *His True Art of Defence* (1594) besides Saviolo's *Practice.* She says Shakespeare was familiar with material in these books and may even have known Saviolo and Segar ("Codes of Violence," p. 86).

7. See Keith Wrightson, *English Society, 1580–1680* (New Brunswick, N.J.: Rutgers University Press, 1982), pp. 71–74. Wrightson notes that the goodwill of all concerned was nevertheless important; in the first instance, Capulet asks Paris to win Juliet's heart, as his "will to her consent is but a part" (1.2.17).

8. See Peter Laslett, *The World We Have Lost Further Explored,* 3rd ed. (London: Methuen, 1983), pp. 81–91. The information in this paragraph is indebted to Laslett, unless otherwise noted.

9. David Cressy, *Birth, Marriage, and Death: Ritual, Religion, and the Life-Cycle in Tudor and Stuart England* (Oxford: Oxford University Press, 1997), p. 312: "In England a male was legally old enough to be married at the age of 14, a female at the age of 12, but teenage marriages were extremely rare. Most couples waited until their mid-to-late twenties."

10. Laslett comes close to admitting as much: "There is a fairly remote chance, perhaps one out of every hundred or more, that Juliet would have been capable of accepting Romeo's advances, considering that she was a very exceptional young lady, in her diet and general living standards, even if she could not possibly have borne a child by then. But the chances against *both* Juliet *and* her mother having been able to behave in the way we are asked to suppose have to be reckoned in the thousands" (*World We Have Lost*, p. 85). On Juliet's age, see also Chapter 4 herein.

11. R. B. Outhwaite, *Clandestine Marriage in England, 1500–1850* (London: Hambleton Press, 1995), p. 22.

12. Ibid., p. 58. Outhwaite says that from the twelfth to the eighteenth century, clandestine marriage was the only way marriages between men from age fourteen and women from age twelve could be valid against pressures from the outside world, as argued by A. Macfarlane, *Love and Marriage in England, 1300–1840* (Oxford: Oxford University Press, 1986), p. 127. Without this escape hatch, parents could halt the matches of those under the age of twenty-one.

13. See Foster, "Webbing," pp. 141–42, and Joan Ozark Holmer, "No 'Vain Fantasy': Shakespeare's Refashioning of Nashe for Dreams and Queen Mab," in *Texts, Contexts, and Interpretation*, ed. Halio, pp. 49–82. On other debts to Nashe, see Holmer's "Nashe as 'Monarch of Witt' and Shakespeare's *Romeo and Juliet*," *Texas Studies in Literature and Language* 37 (1995): 314–43.

14. See Gayle Whittier, "The Sonnet's Body and the Body Sonnetized in *Romeo and Juliet*," *Shakespeare Quarterly* 40 (1989): 27–41. See also Chapter 5 herein.

15. For sources and analogues relating to Shakespeare's play other than Brooke's poem, see Bullough, ed., *Narrative and Dramatic Sources*, vol. 1, pp. 269–76, and Brian Gibbons's New Arden edition (London: Methuen, 1980), pp. 32–37.

16. To cite but one example: In his passion for Rosaline, Romeo's "posturing and oxymoronic excess" demonstrates the fashionable Renaissance love-melancholy, as well as certain Petrarchanisms and other motifs of the courtly love and sonnet traditions. See G. B. Evans, ed., *New Cambridge Shakespeare* (Cambridge: Cambridge University Press, 1984), p. 197, and the discussion of Shakespeare's verse in Chapter 5.

3

DRAMATIC STRUCTURE

OVERVIEW

For Shakespeare's plays, as for all Elizabethan drama, the scene was the basic building block, or unit, for his dramatic design.[1] His work nevertheless reveals a discernable overall pattern, or architecture, that is equally significant. Like *Richard II*, written within the same two- or three-year period, *Romeo and Juliet* pivots in the middle, balancing some scenes in the first half with comparable scenes in the second. The pivot occurs with the death of Mercutio (3.1).[2] What seemed to be a largely comic invention turns at that point to tragedy, Romeo's presentiments in 1.4 fully borne out.[3] On the other hand, comic elements so much in evidence earlier do not entirely disappear from the second half, not only in the scene with Peter and the musicians (4.5.100–138), but also in the dialogue between the Nurse and Old Capulet (e.g., 4.4.5–10). Shakespearean drama, again like much of his contemporaries' work—but unlike classical or later neoclassical drama—freely mixed genres to reflect more comprehensively the totality of human experience.[4]

The comic element in this tragedy does more. As Maynard Mack suggests, it helps distance the audience from the tragic action as it unwinds, but it does not appear relentless.[5] On the contrary, somewhat like Shakespeare's later and greater tragedy *King Lear*, several events seem to promise a happy outcome—the triumph of comedy over tragedy—only to come crashing down at the end into catastrophe.[6] Instead of condemning Romeo to death—the sentence Prince Escalus had promised all those who broke Verona's peace (1.1.87–88)—he banishes him. In this fashion Escalus opens the way, as Friar Lawrence sees it (3.3.150–54)—and with him, we the audience—for Romeo's future pardon. Later, when her father demands that Juliet marry Paris, Friar Lawrence again comes to the rescue with a potion that promises to buy the lovers time and prevent Juliet's threatened suicide. The comic scenes that immediately follow Juliet's taking the potion enhance this expectation of a happier outcome. Shakespeare leads us on—not unlike the "flattering truth of sleep" that leads Romeo to expect "some joyful news at hand" at the beginning 5.1. In so doing, he makes the final outcome appear much more tragic, juxtaposing the harsh reality of events against the common human tendency to hope.

Along with this blending of comedy and tragedy is the balancing of certain scenes. The preparations for the ball in 1.2, for example, finds its counterpart in 4.2, as Old Capulet again sends his servant to invite guests to the feast. Similarly, Juliet's forebodings at 3.5.51, 54–57 echo Romeo's presentiments at 1.4.106. Friar Lawrence's counsel to Juliet in 3.4 parallels his to Romeo in 2.3. Juliet's impatience to receive Romeo as her husband in 3.2 parallels her eagerness to hear the news from the Nurse regarding Romeo's intentions in 2.5. In both scenes the Nurse comes with important news, but her news, comically delayed in 2.5, contrasts sharply with the message she delivers concerning Tybalt's death in act 3. Again, Juliet confides in her Nurse in both 2.5 and 3.5, but the advice she receives from her confidante in the latter scene concerning marriage to Paris affects Juliet quite differently. Juliet meets Romeo in Friar Lawrence's cell in 2.6, but their meeting is quite different from that between Juliet and Paris in 4.1 in the same place. Finally, though their substance and function are different, Mercutio's Queen Mab speech in 1.4 and Juliet's vision of the tomb in 4.3 show the same qualities of vivid imagination and appear to parallel each other in their respective parts of the play.[7]

It would be wrong, however, to view *Romeo and Juliet* as simply Shakespeare's balancing act, just as it would be to view *Richard II* in that way. Across (or within) the meaningful network of parallels and contrasts, the narrative movement progresses vigorously, all of its twists and turns notwithstanding. Or rather, the convolutions of the plot, abetted by the secondary but nonetheless important subplot involving Paris's suit for Juliet (or Romeo's for Rosaline), lend a rich complexity to Shakespeare's drama. If the course of true love never did run smooth, as Lysander advises Hermia in *A Midsummer Night's Dream* (1.1.134), Shakespeare shows how rocky and treacherous the terrain really can be in this play compared to that in his lyrical comedy.

An alternative way of viewing the overall structure of *Romeo and Juliet* is to see it as comprising several movements, each beginning or ending with dawn, only the last one coinciding with Nicholas Rowe's inserted act division.[8] The first begins at dawn and ends after 9:00 A.M., as Romeo's conversation with Benvolio concludes (1.1.229). The second begins that evening (1.2) with the preparations for the Capulets' ball and ends as dawn breaks and Romeo and Juliet bid each other good-night (2.2.189). The next and longest movement begins immediately afterward at dawn the same day with Friar Lawrence's soliloquy and finishes that night after Tybalt and Mercutio are dead, the Friar and Nurse minister to Romeo's despair (3.3), and Capulet and Paris make plans for Paris's marriage to Juliet (3.4). The fourth movement begins at dawn the next day, after Romeo and Juliet consummate their marriage, speak their aubade, and separate (3.5). The movement continues as

Juliet learns that she must marry Paris, seeks counsel of Friar Lawrence, and takes the potion he gives her (4.4). This movement ends as dawn approaches, the Capulet household is busy preparing for the wedding, Paris and the musicians arrive, and Juliet is found lying lifeless on her bed (4.5). The last movement covers the period during which Romeo learns of Juliet's entombment, returns to Verona, kills Paris and himself, and Juliet awakens and also commits suicide. The movement—and the play—ends with the final dawn, the "glooming peace this morning brings," that Prince Escalus announces.[9]

SHAKESPEARE'S DRAMATIC DEVICES

Juxtaposition of scenes—the way back-to-back scenes or those in close proximity served to comment on, parallel, or contrast with each other—was an important method of Elizabethan drama, and Shakespeare made great use of this device. In 1.1, for example, the Montagues voice their concern to Benvolio about their son's melancholy. Like a good parent, Montague worries about his child, fearing that his affliction (from whatever cause) may blight him permanently. In 1.2, Juliet's father—Montague's counterpart—shows concern for his child, negotiating for his daughter's marriage with Count Paris, but here not as eager as he will be later to consummate a deal with the Count until he is sure that Juliet is agreeable to the match. Both scenes thus introduce the hero and heroine of the play, before we actually encounter them, as a son and a daughter. And not just any son and daughter, but the only children of the feuding families that have brought on the furious fight of the play's opening scene.[10]

Whether we regard 2.1 and 2.2 as one continuous scene or not—the couplet that connects them indicates that Shakespeare saw no break here[11]—their juxtaposition becomes highly meaningful, especially if one asks with Harold Goddard, "Why does Shakespeare place the extreme example of [Mercutio's] soiled fantasies precisely before the balcony scene?"[12] This sort of question invariably helps uncover the design of Shakespeare's dramatic structure and its significance—the relation, that is, of form and meaning in the play. Goddard answers his question (and ours, too, if we approach the play with an inquiring attitude): by placing Mercutio's bawdy talk immediately before Romeo's encounter with Juliet, Shakespeare stresses the freedom from sensuality in Romeo's passion as distinguished from his friend's far more carnal preoccupations and proclivities. The distinction is important and complements another important contrast, that between Romeo's initial infatuation with Rosaline and his later, more profound love for Juliet.

One of the most significant juxtapositions in the play again involves Mercutio. It occurs at the end of 2.6, as Friar Lawrence brings the two young lovers to the marriage altar, and the beginning of 3.1, when Mercutio and Benvolio enter, "swords on hip, armed servants following them, Mercutio with mischief enough a-bubble in him" for the prudent Benvolio to beg him to retire.[13] Whereas 2.6 begins with the Friar's invocation to the heavens to smile upon the holy act of matrimony that is about to take place, 3.1 begins with Benvolio's worry: "The day is

hot, and Capulets abroad" and "the mad blood stirring." The violence that concerns Benvolio very swiftly breaks out, and Romeo's attempts to promote peace
nothing avail; instead, he earns his friend's curse upon "both your houses," Mercutio having been hurt under his arm (3.1.90–94).

Within scenes, too, juxtapositions can be significant. In the midst of Friar
Lawrence's soliloquy that begins 2.3, Romeo enters. His entrance is interestingly
framed:

> For naught so vile, that on the earth doth live,
> But to the earth some special good doth give;
> Nor ought so good but, strained from that fair use,
> Revolts from true birth, stumbling on abuse.
> Virtue itself turns vice, being misapplied,
> And vice sometime by action dignified.
>
> *Enter* ROMEO.
>
> With the infant rind of this weak flower
> Poison hath residence, and medicine power. (ll. 17–24)

Friar Lawrence is of course talking about the herbs and plants that he is gathering
in his "osier cage," or basket, and is unaware of Romeo's approach and entrance,
but in the broader context of the play's action and its ambiguities, his comments
take on greater resonance. Romeo and Juliet impetuously falling in love and secretly getting married may, in some sense, be a vice, a dereliction of duty to their
parents. But the "vice" may sometimes convert to good, as the Friar later recognizes when he sees the good that Romeo and Juliet's marriage may do to reconcile
the families (ll. 91–92). The "baleful weeds" mentioned earlier (l. 8), however
"vile," may yet have some "special good" to give, which anticipates the potion
Friar Lawrence gives Juliet to help her out of her predicament (4.1.68–76). But
naturally good substances, perverted from their proper use, may end in abuse, like
the poison the Apothecary gives to Romeo in act 5.[14]

Whereas the individual scene typically acts as a unit, some scenes are more
complex in design and may actually comprise several such units. These might be
called "portmanteau scenes," insofar as they convey more than a single function,
or comprise the action of several short scenes linked together as one. The first
scene in *Romeo and Juliet* is such a portmanteau scene. It begins with the dialogue
between Sampson and Gregory and quickly proceeds to the quarrel with Abraham
and soon a general melee between the Montagues and the Capulets. The Prince's
entrance and speech mark a pivotal moment, quelling the riot and leading to the
dialogue between Benvolio and Romeo's parents. This dialogue, in turn, is succeeded by that between Benvolio and Romeo, where the action of the beginning of
1.1—"Here's much to do with hate"—contrasts strikingly with Romeo's preoccupation with love (164 ff.). Thus within a single scene, swung around by Prince
Escalus's appearance, love and hate—the principal subjects of the play—are juxtaposed.

Act 1, scene 2 is also a portmanteau scene and presents other significant juxta-positions. It begins with Paris's suit to Juliet's father, pivots on the Servant's diffi-culty in reading the list of those invited to the feast that Capulet has given him, and then focuses on Romeo and Benvolio. Benvolio is in the midst of advising his friend to forget Rosaline by taking "some new infection to thy eye" (1. 48). Paris is thereby juxtaposed against Romeo, both of whom become Juliet's suitors and both of whom eventually die as a result of their love for her.[15]

Although modern editions usually mark a scene division at the end of 4.3, when Juliet drinks the potion and falls upon her bed, the early quartos show the action to be continuous. In this sense, 4.3–4.4 also make a portmanteau scene, one that in-cludes a juxtaposition of striking dramatic effect and one that Shakespeare clearly intended. As the action was presented on the Elizabethan stage, after "Juliet falls upon the bed, within the curtains,"[16] the audience remained conscious of the bed and what lay hidden by its curtains during everything that immediately follows: the Capulets preparing for the next day's wedding feast, servants coming and going, Paris's bridal music playing, the Nurse's bawdy talk as she tries to waken Juliet and then draws back the curtains to find the young woman lying there stark and still. It is one of the chief dramatic effects of the play, as Harley Granville-Barker says (*Prefaces*, p. 63), and can be gained only by preserving the continuity of the action, instead of breaking it up by an unnecessary and un-Shakespearean scene division.

Another staple of Elizabethan and Shakespearean drama was the soliloquy, and several important soliloquies occur in *Romeo and Juliet*. These serve to let us, the audience, know what the character is thinking and feeling, in much the same way that today's television drama voice-overs function. In this convention of Elizabethan stagecraft, usually the characters are alone on stage, or they be-lieve they are; even when some other character or characters are on stage, none hears what the speaker says in soliloquy.[17] Among the most famous soliloquies in this play are Juliet's in 2.5, 3.2, and 4.3, already mentioned, and Romeo's at the beginning of the first balcony scene (2.2.1–25) and in the last act, when he determines to join Juliet in the tomb (5.1.34–55) and after he kills Paris and takes the poison (5.3.74–120). Shakespeare expends some of his best and most powerful poetry in these speeches, as befits the occasions, and demonstrates the devotion and integrity of the lovers in their willingness to give their lives for each other.

In some instances, what a character may have intended as a soliloquy is in fact overheard by another character. This is precisely what happens in 1.5 when Tybalt overhears Romeo's apostrophe to Juliet's beauty and at once recognizes him as a Montague. Fortunately, Old Capulet is too good a host to allow Tybalt to confront Romeo at that moment, although, being the angry young man he is, Tybalt later is-sues a challenge that precipitates both Mercutio's death and his own, as well as Romeo's banishment. Similarly, Romeo violates Elizabethan dramatic convention in 2.2 when he overhears Juliet speaking in presumed soliloquy of her love for him (ll. 33–51).[18] Shakespeare therefore is not utterly bound by the conventions of his drama, or rather, he will deliberately break a convention for another intended dramatic effect.[19]

Among the less important dramatic devices Shakespeare uses in this play is stychomythia, or the rapid repartee between two characters, usually consisting of a line of dialogue each in quick succession. The dialogue between Juliet and Paris (4.1.18–36) is a good example of this device. The two characters have not actually met until now, and it is a painfully awkward moment for Juliet, who has been promised to Paris by her father. To cover her feelings of repulsion, she takes on Paris's sophisticated tone, briskly denying his claims and disclaiming his compliments.[20] Her formal manner contrasts sharply a few moments later with the language she uses when speaking with Friar Lawrence. Shakespeare is adept in shifting varieties of dialogue and tones of utterance for dramatic as well as poetic effect, as this scene demonstrates.

Of the two Choruses in the play, we need say little. The first provides the context for the action of the play and overemphasizes the role of fate, or fortune, in the tragedy, although it rightly stresses the sacrifice the young lovers make with their lives to bury the ancient hatred between their families.[21] It begins by remarking that both the Houses of Montague and Capulet are "alike in dignity," that is, have equal social status and honor in Verona: neither one nor the other enjoys any kind of advantage or claim upon our sympathy or partiality. The sonnet form of the Chorus anticipates the sonnets and near sonnets that later appear in the dialogue and the abundance of rhyme and formal speech that characterizes the first half of the play.[22] The second Chorus is far less significant and in fact is dispensed with altogether in Q1, as in most modern productions.[23] Samuel Johnson's comment on it is frequently quoted: "The use of this chorus is not easily discovered; it conduces nothing to the progress of the play, but relates what is already known, or what the next scene will show; and relates it without adding the improvement of any moral sentiment."[24]

THE LINKS BETWEEN PLOT AND SUBPLOTS

Although *Romeo and Juliet* has no fully formed double- or treble-plot, as do *A Midsummer Night's Dream* and *Much Ado about Nothing*, to cite only two examples from among Shakespeare's plays, it does contain two important if rudimentary subplots. In this, it more closely resembles *Macbeth*, for instance, where the Cawdor plot, developed briefly in the first act, in some ways anticipates and contrasts with the main action of the drama. Romeo's infatuation with Rosaline is just such a subplot, used here to contrast with his later, more fully developed love for Juliet. When Romeo first appears, he looks and sounds like a typical distraught lover (in Elizabethan terms),[25] mooning over a woman who steadfastly refuses to yield to Romeo's suit. Rosaline will "not be hit / With Cupid's arrow," he complains to Benvolio:

> she hath Dian's wit;
> And in strong proof of chastity well armed,

From Love's weak childish bow she lives uncharmed.
She will not stay the siege of loving terms,
Nor bide th'encounter of assailing eyes,
Nor ope her lap to saint-seducing gold.
O, she is rich in beauty, only poor
That when she dies, with beauty dies her store. (1.1.200–207)

These are the accents and the terms familiar to Shakespeare's audience from the Petrarchan sonneteers, who enjoyed great popularity in the 1590s, at the time when Shakespeare was writing *Romeo and Juliet*. The cold, chaste mistress had become a stereotype by then; hence, Romeo's love for Rosaline smacks of the artificial, the conventional, not something deep and moving. It is to get his friend out of this melancholy, lovelorn state that Benvolio suggests in the next scene that they go to the Capulets' party, where Romeo will see Rosaline in the context of other beauties who will make this "swan" look like a "crow" by comparison (1.2.82–87).

That is precisely what happens, of course, despite Romeo's initial skepticism and the reassertion of his devotion to Rosaline. As soon as he sees Juliet, he is captivated by her: "O she doth teach the torches to burn bright!" (1.5.43). Not only does his imagery become more concrete and fresh, but he experiences a revolution in his emotion: "Did my heart love till now? forswear it, sight! / For I ne'er saw true beauty till this night" (1.5.51–52). Shakespeare is here using the convention of love at first sight, true enough; moreover, Romeo and Juliet begin speaking with each other in sonnets![26] But this is merely the preamble to the deeper love, conveyed in the more direct and unstudied language they use in their soliloquies and in their dialogue in 2.2. The courtly language disappears; simplicity and candor replace it, as in Juliet's monosyllabic line, followed by Romeo's:

JULIET   I would not for the world they saw you here.

ROMEO   I have night's cloak to hide me from their eyes,
And but thou love me, let them find me here. (2.2.74–76)

Juliet admits soon afterward that if Romeo had not already overheard her in her supposed soliloquy, she might have played her part differently; "but farewell compliment," she says, and asks with disarming innocence: "Dost thou love me?" (1. 90).[27]

On the other hand, Juliet is not so naive not to know what Romeo's answer will be. The point is—and this is the significant contrast to the subplot—Juliet will have Romeo, but only as her husband. From Romeo's remarks earlier concerning his feelings for Rosaline, marriage is not quite what he had in mind there. That was never the issue in courtly love, the discourse of which he emulates, in any case. But it is the issue for Shakespeare's more serious lovers, from first to last, from *The Two Gentlemen of Verona* and *The Comedy of Errors* to *The Winter's Tale* and *The Tempest*.

That is the issue, also, for the other subplot involving the County Paris. A sincere suitor, he wants to marry Juliet, not simply lie with her, and he presses his suit, quite properly, to her father—even before approaching the object of his love. That is a further contrast with the main plot. Although Capulet at first advises Paris to win his daughter's affection, he later decides to make the match even before consulting Juliet. While there is no need to question Paris's love for Juliet, which is not the same as Romeo's for Rosaline, it is a one-sided love, quite unlike the love between the main characters. Shakespeare has Romeo pay tribute to Paris at the end, after Romeo fatally wounds him, to signal that Paris was not an unworthy lover, but "One writ with me in sour misfortune's book" (5.3.82).

Overarching all the action of the play, and in one sense its alternative main plot, is the feud between the rival families. The cause of the feud is lost in the abyss of time.[28] It is within this context that the lovers find themselves doomed, though doom is not quite what they hope for or expect, despite their several presentiments and forebodings. Here Juliet's cousin, Tybalt, and Romeo's friend, Mercutio, play their respective, important roles, as neither of them is willing to overlook a slight or forgo the opportunity for a fight. Both are motivated by a masculine code of honor, scarcely outdated among certain groups—like inner-city street gangs— even today.[29] However scoffing Mercutio may be of codes and conventions, as in his teasing of love-struck Romeo in 1.4 and 2.4, or the formulas of fencing, about which he mocks Tybalt in 3.1, he is as deeply implicated in the ideology that governs the feud as anyone else.[30] Only with the deaths of the young lovers, precipitated in large part by the deaths of Tybalt and Mercutio, is the feud—and with it, this aspect of the plot—finally resolved.

NOTES

1. Act and scene divisions are not marked in the early quartos of *Romeo and Juliet* or in the First Folio text. Nicholas Rowe first inserted them in his edition (1709), followed by subsequent editors, with some variation in scene if not act division. For a discussion of the appropriateness of Rowe's divisions, see Harley Granville-Barker, *Prefaces to Shakespeare*, 4 vols. (1930; rpt. London: Batsford, 1963), vol. 4, pp. 69–73.

2. See Susan Snyder, "*Romeo and Juliet*: Comedy into Tragedy," *Essays in Criticism* 20 (1970): 391–402; reprinted in *Shakespeare's Early Tragedies*, ed. Mark Rose (Englewood Cliffs, N.J.: Prentice-Hall, 1995), 106–14. Snyder further develops the ideas in this essay in her book *The Comic Matrix of Shakespeare's Tragedies* (Princeton, N.J.: Princeton University Press, 1979), esp. pp. 56–73.

3. Cp. Michael Goldman, *Shakespeare and the Energies of Drama* (Princeton, N.J.: Princeton University Press, 1972), pp. 41–42: "*Romeo and Juliet* . . . has clear affinities with the Shakespearean comedies of its period. Except for its fatalities, it follows the standard form of New Comedy. The two lovers are kept apart by a powerful external authority (some form of parental opposition is typical), and much of the action concerns their efforts to get around the obstacles put in their path. Their ultimate union—in a marriage feast—results in a transformation of the society that has opposed them."

4. Cp. Franklin M. Dickey, *Not Wisely but Too Well* (San Marino: Huntington Library, 1957), p. 65, who cites Cinthio's theory justifying the alternation of comic and tragic scenes in the same play.

5. Maynard Mack, "The Ambiguities of *Romeo and Juliet*," in Maynard Mack, *Everybody's Shakespeare* (Lincoln: University of Nebraska Press, 1993), pp. 69, 83.

6. See my section on "Promised and Disappointed Endings," in *King Lear*, ed. Jay L. Halio (Cambridge: Cambridge University Press, 1992), pp. 29–33, and Stephen Booth, *"King Lear," "Macbeth," Indefinition, and Tragedy* (New Haven, Conn.: Yale University Press, 1983), pp. 5–20. Snyder, *Comic Matrix*, takes a different view of events in *Romeo and Juliet*: "In Mercutio's sudden, violent end, Shakespeare makes the birth of tragedy coincide exactly with the symbolic death of comedy" (p. 62). For her, as for Romeo (3.1.110–11), an irreversible process has begun, although she later notes (pp. 66–67) how the possibilities of comedy persist later on.

7. Cp. Stanley Wells, "The Challenges of *Romeo and Juliet*," *Shakespeare Survey* 49 (1996): 5, who notes other parallels as evidence of Shakespeare's formal patterning.

8. See Brian Gibbons's New Arden edition of the play (London: Methuen, 1960), pp. 54–55.

9. Cp. ibid. with the time scheme in the play as analyzed by G. B. Evans in the *New Cambridge Shakespeare* (Cambridge: Cambridge University Press, 1984), pp. 10–11.

10. See Susan Snyder, "Ideology and the Feud in *Romeo and Juliet*," *Shakespeare Survey* 49 (1996): 87–96.

11. In her forthcoming Oxford edition, Jill Levenson does not break the scene in two.

12. Harold Goddard, *The Meaning of Shakespeare* (Chicago: University of Chicago Press, 1951), p. 122.

13. Thus Granville-Barker describes their entrance, commenting on the contrast with the scene of "quiet consummation" immediately preceding (see *Prefaces,* vol. 4, p. 51). He calls the scene that follows "the most strikingly effective thing in the play" (p. 52) and in a footnote refers to the contrast between scenes, swiftly succeeding each other, Shakespeare's "chief technical resource."

14. See also Goldman, *Energies of Drama,* pp. 38–39.

15. Other portmanteau scenes include 1.5 (especially if 1.4 is not taken as a separate scene), 2.4, 3.1, 3.5, 4.1, 4.5, 5.1, and 5.3. In some editions, for example, the *Everyman Shakespeare,* ed. John Andrews (New York: Dutton, 1993), 4.3–4.5 are treated as a single portmanteau scene.

16. This is the Q1 stage direction, adopted by most modern editions, although they end the scene here. But on the Elizabethan stage, the bed was not withdrawn; it remained in view throughout 4.4. Modern productions that drop the curtain at this point destroy the dramatic effect Shakespeare intended in what follows.

17. Compare *Hamlet* 3.1, where Ophelia is on stage during Hamlet's "To be or not to be" soliloquy. Although some recent productions show Hamlet speaking directly to Ophelia, this evidently was not Shakespeare's intended staging of the scene.

18. See Harry Levin, "Form and Formality in *Romeo and Juliet*," *Shakespeare Quarterly* 4 (1960): 3–11; reprinted in *"Romeo and Juliet": Critical Essays*, ed. John F. Andrews (New York: Garland, 1993), pp. 41–53. References are to the reprint.

19. For further discussion of the soliloquies in *Romeo and Juliet*, see Larry S. Champion, *Shakespeare's Tragic Perspective* (Athens: University of Georgia Press, 1976), pp. 76–80. Champion analyzes their narrative and rhetorical emphases, noting how they help

develop close rapport between the characters and the audience but do not establish a level of dramatic conflict, as they do, for example, in *Hamlet*.

20. Levin, "Form and Formality," p. 43.

21. For discussion of the role of the Chorus in this play and in *Henry V* and *Troilus and Cressida*, see Goddard, *Meaning of Shakespeare*, pp. 118, 216–17. Goddard argues that the Chorus in this play and in the others does not speak with the author's voice. See also Jill Levenson's commentary on the Prologue in her Oxford edition of *Romeo and Juliet*.

22. As Evans notes (*New Cambridge Shakespeare,* p. 53), the verse form was probably suggested by the "Argument," an Italian sonnet, prefacing Arthur Brooke's poem.

23. In the Folio, both Choruses are omitted. See E. Pearlman, "Shakespeare at Work: *Romeo and Juliet*," *English Literary Renaissance* 24 (1994): 320–27, who argues that Shakespeare changed his mind in the course of writing his tragedy and presumably dropped his original play to introduce each act with a chorus, as did many other tragedies in the period 1580–1595 (e.g., Thomas Kyd's *The Spanish Tragedy*).

24. Quoted by Evans, ed., *New Cambridge Shakespeare,* p. 88, in whose edition the Chorus concludes act 1 instead of serving as a prologue to act 2. Cp. Granville-Barker, *Prefaces,* vol. 4, p. 70, who sees a possible mechanical function for the Chorus in staging the following scene.

25. Cp. Rosalind's description of a lover in *As You Like It* (3.2.370–81) and Ophelia's description of the distraught Hamlet in *Hamlet* (2.1.74–80).

26. Cp. Granville-Barker, *Prefaces*, vol. 4, p. 48. Granville-Barker sees "something sacramental" in this meeting ceremony, something unlike the kindling of passion common to "the cheapest of tragedies." It is, rather, "something grave and sweet; it is a marriage made already."

27. Cp. Levin, "Form and Formality," p. 43.

28. Cp. Snyder, "Ideology and the Feud," p. 88: "Like ideology . . . the feud has no obvious genesis that can be discerned, no history. It pervades everything, not as a set of specific ideas but as repeated practices."

29. This point is evidenced in *West Side Story*, a modern adaptation of *Romeo and Juliet*, as well as in the recent film version set in Verona, Florida.

30. Snyder, "Ideology and the Feud," p. 92.

4

CHARACTERS

The characters in *Romeo and Juliet* tend to divide into two groups along generational lines. In fact, a conflict of generations—the different ways of viewing the world and of acting in it—lies close to the heart of this tragedy, as in many plays, mostly comedies. Commentators have often remarked on the affinities of *Romeo and Juliet* with the Italian commedia dell'arte—the *senex*, for example, the old man, father of the young man (or woman) who tries to prevent the lovers' union, the young lovers themselves, the clever servant, and so forth.[1] Moreover, in attempting to make a tragedy out of romantic love—as opposed to the classical subjects advocated and adopted since Aristotle first formulated the qualities of the tragic personages in his *Poetics*—Shakespeare was engaging in something innovative and experimental.[2] Not kings or princes—the protagonists of high tragedy as usually conceived—but the young scions of noble houses were his principal characters. And arrayed for or against them were others, young and old, who abetted or deterred their love.

THE OLDER GENERATION

To begin with, the characters of the older generation in *Romeo and Juliet*: Note at once that they are not all of a type. The elder Montagues and Capulets are different from Friar Lawrence, for example, and all of them are different again from the Nurse. While they share many prejudices as well as comic behaviors, Old Montague and Old Capulet are not identical, just as their wives, too, are different from each other, though both show concern for their husbands during the brawl in 1.1. Lady Capulet has a larger role than her counterpart, whom we hear very briefly asking about her son (1.1.107–8), and who appears but does not speak in 3.1, after Romeo has killed Tybalt. At the end of the play, we hear that she has died of grief over her son's banishment (5.3.210–11). Lady Capulet, on the other hand, although also concerned for her child, is uncomfortable talking with her daughter about marriage in 1.3 and later shows little patience with her in act 4, behaving angrily when Juliet refuses at first to marry Paris. Her extreme grief over Tybalt's death and her determination to wreak vengeance upon Romeo (3.5.80–92) has led some stage directors to suggest more than a filial devotion between them. Although by the end of the play she seems nearly crushed by all the mischances that have occurred (5.3.206–7), the contrast between her and Lady Montague remains strong.

Similarly, Juliet's father has a larger role in the tragedy than Montague, and we see more than one side to him. On first appearance, he shows proper paternal regard for his young daughter, who is not quite fourteen years old (1.2.8–19).[3] His concern parallels Montague's for his son in the scene preceding, but his speaking voice is different, not only because of his rhymed couplets. He takes everything rather more casually, being preoccupied with the feast he is holding that evening, to which he invites the young Paris, Juliet's suitor. At the feast, another side to his character emerges, that of the genial host, genial even as regards the gate crashers—Romeo included, Romeo especially. For when Tybalt threatens to disrupt the festivities, Capulet knows how to be round with him and effectively prevents a brawl from breaking out.

To this extent, both Montague and Capulet reflect what, in a later play, one of Shakespeare's characters refers to as the manners of a "golden age."[4] But after Tybalt's death and Romeo's banishment, their attitudes and actions change. Montague intercedes on behalf of his son, but ineffectually (3.1.175–77); Lady Capulet is far more strident than he (ll. 167–72). Capulet has nothing to say, though later he changes his position concerning Juliet's marriage and concludes with Paris a match on the spot—despite the fact that he has been unable so far to consult his daughter's own wishes in the matter (3.4).[5] His outrage at her demurrer (3.5.141–95), which almost moves him to violence, prompts his wife as well as the Nurse to intervene. This is the irate father of comedy, but his tone changes once more when he sees Juliet's inert body on her bed afterward, and he is moved to utter a deeply felt tribute to her youth and beauty: "Death lies on her like an untimely frost / Upon the sweetest flower of all the field" (4.5.28–29). At the very end, after both Romeo and Juliet lie truly dead, he is able to clasp hands with his "brother Montague" and recognize with him "Poor sacrifices of our enmity!" (5.3.303–4). The benevolence and generosity that underlie their characters from the first now break forth in this simultaneous recognition and tribute and the need for reconciliation.

Two other characters of their generation also require attention: Friar Lawrence and the Nurse. Although Arthur Brooke's poem presents the Friar contemptuously—a reflection of the author's antipapist convictions—Shakespeare makes him a far more sympathetic character. It is to his kindly good counsel that both Romeo and later Juliet turn when they find themselves in a seemingly hopeless predicament, and they leave not unsatisfied, but reassured and hopeful. The Friar first appears in his function as moral commentator, or chorus, gathering herbs, plants, and stones for their medicinal purposes, noting not only their healing properties, but also their dangerous qualities when misapplied or abused (2.3.7–20). He further generalizes by alluding to a similar ambiguity in human nature (ll. 21–22, 27–30). The irony of his discourse becomes apparent only later when his plan involving the potion he gives to Juliet backfires.

When Romeo enters, Friar Lawrence shows his sympathetic understanding of the young man and does so with engaging humor. He immediately perceives that although it is now early morning, Romeo has not yet been to bed. When he teases Romeo about Rosaline, Romeo informs his confessor that he no longer thinks of her but has fallen in love with Juliet. The Friar is surprised at this news and twits Romeo about his fickleness (ll. 65–80). But he is soon able to put his humor and his remonstrations aside as he glimpses a possible positive outcome of an alliance between the two young lovers. For this reason, although he cautions that "they stumble that run fast" (l. 94), he is willing—perhaps too quickly willing—to accept as fact the reciprocal love between the two young people. In this, as in some of his other actions—for example, the solution he proposes to Juliet in act 4—he appears to some critics as given to acting precipitously.[6]

The action most damaging to the Friar, however, occurs in the final scene, when he hears the Watch approach and hurries away from Juliet, leaving her alone in the tomb with the body of Romeo aslant upon her. But, as G. B. Evans argues, Shakespeare probably did not intend thereby to reveal a lurking weakness in the Friar's character. He was more likely concentrating on what must have appeared as a dramatic necessity—that is, the need to present Juliet at this crucial moment in "symbolic isolation."[7] But why have the Friar enter the scene at all? Apart from the plot requirement—that he inform Juliet that their plan has gone awry and they must leave the tomb—dramatic necessity also seems to dictate that the Watch apprehend the Friar moments later so that he can deliver the final untangling of all that has so far transpired.

When the Friar's long speech and much else at the end of the play is often curtailed in modern productions, the effect that Shakespeare clearly intended is lost, as Harley Granville-Barker maintains (*Prefaces*, pp. 68–69). The Friar's story must be told, he says, because the play's true end is not the lovers' deaths, but the end of the feud, and the play's "ambiguities," as the Prince calls them (5.3.217), must be cleared up. The Friar's plain tale, furthermore, reemphasizes the "simple pity" of the various mischances and allows this to be the audience's final impression. Insofar as declamation is the "norm" of the play's method, it returns quite naturally to that method. At the end of his long speech, the Friar says he is willing to assume responsibility for what has happened, and if need be, he will pay with his life; but in a gesture of recognition and magnanimity—"We have still known thee for a holy man" (l. 270)—Prince Escalus pardons him. Nevertheless, Granville-Barker admits, this stretch of writing reflects the author's "flagging impulse" and is of relatively poor quality—yet another inducement for stage adapters to wield their blue pencils.

In direct contrast to the Friar, the Nurse appears as a far coarser and earthier character. Often portrayed as a lovable old fool, whose bawdy speeches are designed to amuse and delight us, she is much more than that, and perhaps not primarily that at all. At a crucial point in her development, Juliet sees her for what she truly is: a "most wicked fiend" (3.5.235).[8] But that is not the impression she conveys early in the play, when she goes on about the way she nursed Juliet after her own child, Susan, had died (1.3.13–58). The immediate impression is one merely of worldliness and gross sensuality. For this reason, she has often been compared to Shakespeare's Falstaff, another sensualist, but the resemblance is superficial. For one thing, the Nurse lacks Falstaff's fertile imagination; her long speech about Juliet's childhood, for example, derives only from recollection. As a talker consciously and unconsciously given to bawdry, she is closer to Mercutio, but there, too, she lacks his imaginative ability, and the two hate each other on instinct, as two rival talkers usually do.[9]

The Nurse shows her true colors when Juliet appeals to her for aid and counsel after her parents demand that she marry Paris. Unlike the elder Capulets, the Nurse knows the situation and has indeed abetted Juliet in marrying Romeo and consummating the marriage soon afterward. Aware of Juliet's predicament, then, how does she respond? By telling Juliet to go ahead and commit bigamy—that Romeo is dead or as good as (3.5.224–25)! Sensualist that she is, the Nurse compares Paris and Romeo, "Romeo's a disclout to him," and goes on to praise the other's physical features (3.5.218–23). Worldly as she is, she is also a pragmatist: since Romeo is banished, the odds are he won't come back again to lie with Juliet, or if he does come back, he must do it by stealth—not a happy prospect. Juliet is well advised, therefore, to heed her parents' desire and marry Paris. Having received the Nurse's counsel, is it any wonder that Juliet flies to Friar Lawrence for better?

THE YOUNGER GENERATION

Just as the members of the older generation differ among themselves, so do those of the younger generation—if anything, more markedly—though this is without question a play primarily characterized by young people and young people's feelings and preoccupations. Benvolio, one of the first to appear, most closely resembles his elders, or at least Prince Escalus and the Friar, in being of a more sedate and peace-loving disposition (his very name implies that he is a man of "good will").[10] When the brawl breaks out in 1.1, he attempts to stop the fighting and appeals to Tybalt to help him (ll. 55–60). He is soundly rebuffed by the latter, who enjoys nothing more than a good fight, and so the two duel until others enter and join in the fray and the Prince finally stops it. As he does again in 3.1, Benvolio accounts to Escalus and his uncle, Old Montague, what has happened (ll. 97–106). His description of events shows that while he is averse to fighting, he is no coward: meeting Tybalt's challenge, he interchanged thrusts and blows until the Prince arrived. Later, at the beginning of 3.1, he tries to get Mercutio to retire, since the day is hot, the Capulets are abroad, and with "the mad blood stirring" another brawl seems likely. But he is no more successful then with Mercutio than he was earlier with that other hothead, Tybalt.

Benvolio's character is further developed in his dialogue with his uncle and aunt concerning Romeo. Although we never learn the cause, Benvolio's mind is somehow "troubled" (1.1.111), rendering him insomniac. He therefore sympathizes with Romeo, whom he saw also walking alone in the hours before dawn, and agrees to help find out what troubles him. In the ensuing dialogue, he quickly learns that a lover's melancholy afflicts Romeo, who pours out to him complaints of Rosaline's behavior. Although he rejects Benvolio's advice to "Examine other beauties" (1.1.219) and forget her, and he later scoffs at the idea when his friend again urges the remedy (1.2.44–55), this is of course precisely what happens as soon as Romeo sees Juliet. For better or worse—worse, unfortunately, as events unfold—Benvolio is right.

He is also right in trying to stop Mercutio from fighting with Tybalt "in the public haunt of men," urging them instead to "reason coldly" of their grievances or depart (3.1.43–46)—all to no avail. When Romeo intervenes during their duel, he calls upon Benvolio to help beat down their weapons. What happens at that point until Mercutio falls wounded is unclear. Presumably, as Benvolio is drawing his weapon to assist Romeo, Tybalt strikes the fatal blow and then runs away. When he returns and Romeo confronts him, Benvolio is silent, for like Romeo he realizes— or so we may assume—that retribution for Mercutio's death must follow. When it is over and Tybalt is dead, it is he who explains to the Prince the "unlucky manage of this fatal brawl" (3.1.134). After this scene we never see Benvolio again.[11]

Tybalt is the exact opposite of Benvolio. Fiery tempered and impulsive, he takes very seriously the vendetta that exists between the Houses of Montague and Capulet; he is even willing to disrupt the festivities of the Capulets' party to deal with gate-crashing Romeo (1.5.53–58). Only his uncle's stern admonishment restrains him. But nothing restrains him later from inciting Romeo to fight after he has sent him a challenge by letter (3.1.53–54). By this time, of course, Mercutio's taunts have already roused him—not that his blood, which seems always up, needs much arousing. When Romeo refuses to fight, offering only cryptic excuses, Mercutio becomes incensed and meets the challenge for him.

Just how Tybalt wounds Mercutio is a question that has caused some controversy. All we learn from the text is that Mercutio was hurt under Romeo's arm (3.1.94). Q1's stage direction, "Tibalt under Romeos arme thrusts Mercutio, in and flyes," missing in Q2, complicates matters somewhat, especially if the punctuation is correct. Does Tybalt take unfair advantage of Romeo's interference to thrust at Mercutio, whom until then he has been unable to hit? Is he, as Mercutio describes him, merely "a braggart . . . that fights by the book of arithmetic" (3.1.92–93), that is, a textbook fencer?[12] Or is the thrust that kills Mercutio an accident, as Franco Zeffirelli staged it in his film? If Tybalt is the gentleman he is supposed to be, living by a strict code of honor, he could not be guilty of so cowardly an action as some attribute to him. Furthermore, if he is a coward, why does he return to the scene not long afterward? According to Jerzy Limon, he comes back precisely because he realizes that running away was wrong, a reflex action engendered by his horror at what was actually an accident, not an intentional maneuver.[13] Although

Romeo describes his return as an attempt to gloat "in triumph, and Mercutio slain" (3.1.113), nothing else in the text justifies that interpretation. Tybalt scornfully answers Romeo's challenge; they fight, and Tybalt falls. From that moment on, the world is no longer the same for Romeo—or Juliet.

Besides providing the pivotal incident for this play, Mercutio has another, more important role. As the Nurse offers an earthy perspective on Juliet's romantic love for Romeo, so Mercutio provides a similar perspective on Romeo's. The principal *eiron,* or ironist, in the play, he actively deflates, or tries to deflate, his friend's effusions.[14] What he does not know—and dies not knowing, as Maynard Mack reminds us (*Everybody's Shakespeare,* p. 90)—is that Romeo's love for Rosaline, which he mercilessly mocks, has been superseded by a much more profound, and reciprocated, love for Juliet. If Mercutio's taunts are justified in 1.4, by 2.1 his cynical remarks, no matter how amusing, are misdirected, and his irony doubles back on itself.

Attempting to "conjure" Romeo, who has given him and Benvolio the slip, Mercutio invokes Rosaline's "bright eyes," "her fine foot, straight leg, and quivering thigh, / And the demesnes that there adjacent lie" (2.1.16–20). Elegant as his language is, it is also centered on the purely physical. For to Mercutio, sex is the reality; everything else is merely a disguise, however articulated, to cover that reality.[15] His cynical remarks nevertheless counterbalance the opposite tendency of the lovers, whose love both incorporates and transcends the physical. In this way, Shakespeare provides in the overall context of his play a complex vision of reality, avoiding the sentimentalities of either the cynic or the romantic by including both, playing one off against the other.[16]

For all his scoffing at romantic love, let us not forget that Mercutio is also a poet, as his Queen Mab speech (1.4.53–94) in some sort reveals.[17] The speech is often regarded as a digression—a lyrical outburst that impedes the forward movement of the action—and so it is. As Harold Goddard demonstrates,[18] it serves several functions that have more to do with character and poetry than with dramatic action. For one thing, in exhibiting a "prankish delicacy" and refined sensibility, it shows another side to Mercutio, who emerges as a more complex character than he might otherwise appear. The finer side of a sensualist, though suppressed, is bound to come out, if at all, incidentally, as Goddard says, in just such a digression. The lines are delightful but are more akin to fancy, or fantasy, as Mercutio himself admits (l. 98), than to true imagination. Shakespeare, as we shall see, leaves the poetry of imagination chiefly to his lovers, no matter where else, as here, sparks of fantasy briefly illuminate the darkness.

Like many of Shakespeare's other heroes—Benedick, Prince Hal, Othello, Antony, to name a few from a variety of genres—Romeo first appears after we have already heard something about him. But unlike the heroes just mentioned, Romeo is not presented in a harshly negative way. His parents' worry about him and Benvolio's description of his solitary wanderings invoke our sympathy, and when we meet him, his anguish—artificial as it must seem—is real enough to him. He is the typical Renaissance romantic lover, bemoaning his Cruel Mistress, uttering copybook oxymora (1.1.167–73), and exhibiting all the airs appropriate to his condition.[19] That he is not as far gone as he pretends reveals itself in his question to Benvolio after his first wail: "Dost thou not laugh?" (l. 174). He has at least this much perspective on his condition and his state of mind, which shows a healthy psyche underneath the pose of a love-struck young puppy.

Further evidence of his essential good health comes during his dialogue with Mercutio and Benvolio before entering the Capulets' ball. Insisting at first that he will not dance—"I am not for this ambling; / Being but heavy, I will bear the light" (1.4.11–12)—his wit breaks out, willy-nilly. Before long he is trading quips with that superwit, Mercutio, for whom he is more than merely a straight man. When his friend seems to get carried away in his discourse on Queen Mab—powerfully portrayed by John McEnery as an extreme neurotic in the Zeffirelli film—Romeo shows his care and compassion, stopping him before he goes over the edge (ll. 95–96). If Romeo's forebodings as they enter the hall still sound the note of the dejected lover anticipating an "untimely death" for his "despised life" (ll. 110–11), his allusion to "Some consequence yet hanging in the stars" echoes the "star-crossed lovers" sounded in the Prologue, but he is nonetheless willing to put his fate in the hands of a higher power ("He that hath the steerage of my course" [l. 112]).

What happens next is too well known and understood to require much comment. Romeo is struck by Juliet's beauty and in a stately, almost reverent, fashion woos her in sonnets. A very willing accomplice, Juliet returns his words and his feelings with those of her own. When each one separately discovers the identity of the other, they experience a moment's dismay—in Juliet's case, perhaps even horror—but are nothing daunted. Their mutual maturity has begun, and there is no turning back, as they plight their vows in the exquisite balcony scene that follows in act 2. Granville-Barker aptly summarizes the subsequent events:

> Rosaline's adorer, aping disillusioned age, is hardly to be recognized in the boyishly, childishly happy Romeo that rushes to the Friar's cell. From there he goes to encounter Mercutio, still overflowing with spirits, apt for a bout of nonsense, victorious in it, too. From this and the meeting with the Nurse, back to the cell, to Juliet and the joining of their hands. (*Prefaces*, vol. 4, p. 88)

If all this makes Romeo sound like an impulsive young lover, that is just what he is. But it is love that propels him, not affectation or infatuation, and that makes all the difference, as Shakespeare is at pains to demonstrate by contrasting Romeo's feelings for Juliet with those he had for Rosaline. His love for Juliet, bound by wedlock but not yet consummated, is also what makes him act as he does when Tybalt finds him in act 3 and tries to force him into a duel. Since his marriage is a secret, no one understands why he behaves as he does—not Tybalt, and not Mercutio, who takes up Tybalt's challenge instead to save his friend's honor.[20] When Mercutio dies as a result, Romeo at once sees the situation for what it is and what he must do to restore not only his honor, but his manliness and valor, which Juliet's beauty, he feels, has too much softened (3.1.100–105).

His immediate reaction to killing Tybalt, as he stands over his body, "stern, fated and passive to the next Capulet sword that offers,"[21] is: "O, I am fortune's fool" (3.1.127). Benvolio finally gets him to flee, and where else should he go but to Friar Lawrence's cell? There he exhibits a kind of reversion to immaturity and despair, ready to kill himself, until the Nurse snatches his dagger away.[22] Friar Lawrence at length calms him down by appealing not only to his manliness, but also to his love for Juliet and hers for him, and to the other positive aspects of his situation (3.3.135–40). When the Nurse gives him the ring Juliet has sent him, Romeo at last relents (1. 165), and they plan for his surreptitious visit to her chamber that night.

It is a bittersweet consummation for the lovers; nevertheless, neither of them is willing to relinquish it. Romeo is the first to recognize the need for him to depart, but when, like any good lover, he yields to Juliet's persuasions to stay, she in her turn, fearful of the danger to him, urges him to leave. It is the last time they will ever have a chance to speak with each other, and Shakespeare endows the scene with some of his most enchanting verse. As in their first balcony scene, they are interrupted by the Nurse, representative of the other world, the materialist and practical one, warning of Lady Capulet's approach. The impingement of her world brings the threat of disaster to all that the lovers have moments before experienced and hope to experience again.

Romeo is absent all during act 4, which is devoted entirely to Juliet and the predicament her parents place her in by forcing her to marry Paris. Usually, when Shakespeare removes a protagonist from the stage for any prolonged period of time, he means to signal a change in that character's attitude or disposition, as he does, for example, in *Hamlet* or, nearer to the composition of *Romeo and Juliet*, in *Richard II*.[23] When Romeo reappears at the start of act 5, he seems quieter, more meditative than he has been before, contemplating as he does the strange dream that has unaccountably lifted his spirits (5.1.1–11). His joy, however, is short-lived, for Balthasar soon enters with news of Juliet's burial in "Capels' monument" (1. 18). Romeo at once reverts to his impulsive, passionate self: "Is it e'en so? then I defy you, stars!" (1. 24).[24] With no more than a moment's reflection, he determines to leave that very night to join Juliet in the tomb. His swift thinking recalls the Apothecary from whom he can get the poison for his suicide, and his imagination bodies forth in precise detail both the Apothecary and the exotic contents of his shop (ll. 37–52). Far different now is Romeo's attitude toward himself and his fate: gone is any remnant of self-pity, and if he recognizes himself as a desperate man, he no longer wails in his despair as he did earlier.[25] A new and rather harsh cynicism colors his speech, which reveals something else new in him: a world-weariness that by now he has well earned. Urging the Apothecary to break Mantua's law, he says:

> Famine is in thy cheeks,
> Need and oppression starveth in thy eyes,
> Contempt and beggary hangs upon thy back;

The world is not thy friend, nor the world's law,
The world affords no law to make thee rich;
Then be not poor, but break it and take this. (ll. 69–74)

We have not heard this tone before in anything Romeo has uttered.[26]

When Romeo approaches the tomb, he takes care (like any dutiful son) to send a letter to his father through Balthasar and orders his man to leave, giving him false excuses for opening Juliet's grave and threatening to tear the lad apart if he returns to pry into what is happening (5.3.22–39). This is not quite the tone used earlier in his rage against Tybalt; it is again harsher and more dire in its threat. His tone changes when Paris tries to apprehend him, but when the Count refuses to desist, he returns to the hateful attitude he had adopted moments before—only to change again when he sees who it is he has killed. Romeo has now fully matured and is able to recognize in Paris "One writ with me in sour misfortune's book!" (l. 82). If he dies before learning that Juliet is not really dead—that he is dreadfully mistaken in his action—never mind. His tribute to her is self-reflexive, testimony as much to his integrity as to her beauty. Similarly, in paying tribute to Tybalt, who lies near Juliet in the tomb, he acknowledges the favor he does him now by killing himself with the same hand that ended the other's life (ll. 97–100).

Much has been written about Juliet's extreme youth, which Shakespeare makes more extreme by decreasing her age in Brooke's poem by two years in his play.[27] Apparently younger, also, than her suitors—Paris and probably Romeo—she emphasizes the dichotomy between youth and age that is at the center of this play. As the scenes progress, however, she matures, perhaps even more than Romeo, though the salient aspects of her maturity—her independent spirit, her forthrightness, her courage—manifest themselves from almost the very start. At first appearing to be little more than an obedient daughter to her mother, she also knows with humor how to help stop the Nurse from going on and on in her bawdy talk (1.3.59). A mixture of innocence and worldliness—an innocence "not yet broken by the world"[28]—she quickly learns to fall in love with someone worthy of her devotion and to assert herself and her desires directly, without equivocation. For she will have Romeo, but only as her husband (2.2.143–48).[29] If she is embarrassed by Romeo's having overheard her in soliloquy (ll. 85–87), she is nevertheless glad to forgo coyness and other foolish, light behavior, and she gets right to the point:

Fain would I dwell on form, fain, fain deny
What I have spoke, but farewell compliment.
Dost thou love me? (ll. 88–90)

She knows that Romeo will answer "Ay," so before he can respond, she continues, fully aware of "lovers' perjuries" and other games that lovers play. Where did she get this knowledge? From her mother? Hardly. From the Nurse? Very likely, though Shakespeare does not say. No matter. The main point is that Juliet deserves to displace Rosaline—and shows it in her conversation with Romeo. She is no

Cruel Mistress, no *belle dame sans merci*, playing with her lover's affections for her own gratification. Quite the opposite: she is as deeply in love with Romeo as he is with her and not afraid to admit it, either to him or to herself. Brave girl, Juliet!

Brave, because she is also aware that Romeo is a Montague: "My only love sprung from my only hate," she says after they first meet:

> Too early seen unknown, and known too late!
> Prodigious birth it is to me,
> That I must love a loathed enemy. (1.5.138–40)

Later, try as she may to will away the danger that his name conveys (2.2.33–49), she realizes she cannot: throughout their colloquy in the garden scene, he risks discovery—and with discovery, death—if any of her kinsmen find him there (ll. 64–65). But the two young people are focused on their own discovery—of each other and of the love that has sprung up between them so swiftly as to defy utterly all obstacles. They unhesitatingly pledge themselves decisively and forever.

In all of this, Juliet is as much the wooer as the wooed. Couched though they may be in hyperbole, her words speak what her actions later show:

> My bounty is as boundless as the sea,
> My love as deep; the more I give to thee,
> The more I have, for both are infinite. (2.2.133–35)

Eager to have Romeo for her husband, she promises to send the very next day to find out "Where and what time thou wilt perform the rite" (l. 146), if indeed he means to marry her. But of that there is no question whatever. How could there be? Even before they spoke a word to each other, Romeo knew what a paragon she was (1.5.43–52). True, it is only her beauty that he sees, but as Plato long ago taught and as many Elizabethans believed (or in their writings pretended to believe), inner beauty was reflected in outer loveliness.

Romeo is thoroughly smitten, and rightly so; but we learn along with him that there is much more to Juliet than her external beauty and charm. She is, or becomes, a woman of stature as well. If, in her eagerness in 2.5 to get the Nurse to tell her what Romeo has said, she reveals an impetuosity more characteristic of early teenagers than grown women, by the time she has married Romeo and awaits him that evening, she has matured considerably.[30] Compare her soliloquy at the start of 2.5 with that at the beginning of 3.2. Her anxiety in the former is far more girlish than in latter, as she impatiently awaits the return of the Nurse. And when the Nurse finally arrives, she cannot bear the delay in finding out what the older woman knows. Of course, the Nurse is teasing at the expense of Juliet's exasperation. Juliet is reduced to using every childish ploy she can to extract the news and only succeeds when she grows "hot" and the Nurse has had her fill of fun. At the same time, Juliet's eagerness and anticipation so feed her love for Romeo that in the following scene she can honestly say to him, "my true love is grown to such excess / I cannot sum up sum of half my wealth" (2.6.32–33).

Her excess of love reveals itself fully in 3.2 as she awaits the arrival of her husband, completely unaware as yet of the tragic events that have just occurred. Her innocence now takes on a different hue—the innocence of a willing bride invoking "love-performing Night" (l. 5). This is no longer a teenager, but a married woman awaiting consummation, her fulfillment as a bride. The rhythms of her verse are stronger, and its mood imperative. Her wit is sharp; her imagery concrete and vivid. This is a woman who knows who she is and what she wants, and her impatience, unlike the impatience of 2.5, is the impatience of eager anticipation and expectation, not of childish anxiety. Her specific reference to childhood shows her awareness of the situation—another sign of maturity—as it highlights her feelings:

> So tedious is this day
> As is the night before some festival
> To an impatient child that hath new robes
> And may not wear them. (3.2.28–31)

Her apostrophe to Romeo preceding these lines is the highest tribute to the fullness of her love, anticipating Cleopatra's apostrophe to Antony:[31]

> Come gentle night, come loving black-browed night,
> Give me my Romeo; and when I shall die
> Take him and cut him out in little stars,
> And he will make the face of heaven so fine
> That all the world will be in love with night,
> And pay no worship to the garish sun. (ll. 20–25)

Brian Gibbons's interpretation of this passage is apt: "Juliet quibbles on *death* as also meaning sexual ecstasy: she prays that Romeo may share the experience with her, in death like a rocket soaring up into the night sky and exploding into innumerable stars."[32] This is not the prayer of a mere girl.

But Juliet is in for a shock that threatens to overturn her feelings completely when a few moments later her Nurse enters with news of the duel. As in 2.5, the Nurse delays in bringing out the full facts, for she is upset, not teasing now, and does not quite know how to deliver her news. Juliet understandably errs in thinking Romeo has died, and then is stunned when she learns it is Tybalt, not Romeo, who is dead—dead by Romeo's hand. If at first she recoils in horror, resorting to a series of oxymora to convey her conflicted feelings toward Romeo—"O serpent heart, hid with a flowering face," "Beautiful tyrant, fiend angelical, / Dove-feathered raven, wolvish-ravening lamb" (ll. 73, 75–76)—the Nurse soon brings her up short when she defames Romeo in less ambiguous terms. Juliet reverts to her previous exaltation of Romeo, remembering now that he is her husband and therefore more precious to her than even "her dearest cousin," Tybalt.

But, like Romeo, Juliet now must face the consequences of his banishment, and the contrast between them here and elsewhere has led some critics to raise her above him in their estimation.[33] Like him, she at first rhapsodizes grief stricken over the word *banishment;* but unlike him, she soon recovers herself without the aid of others' prompting (ll. 108–27). She takes comfort in knowing that Romeo will spend at least one night with her. At the end of that night, as dawn breaks, she is naturally reluctant to let Romeo depart, and the two engage in some sad but delightful banter over whether the lark or the nightingale is singing on "yond pomegranate tree" and whether the rising sun or a meteor lights the sky (3.5.1–25). But Juliet again recovers her mature self when she realizes, as Romeo yields to her persuasion, that for him to stay means his death. She then urges his departure, her presentiment that they may never meet again notwithstanding (l. 51).

Romeo gone, the rest of the scene and all of the next act belong to Juliet, who must deal with her parents' decision to marry her to Paris. Playing the hypocrite and deftly countering her mother's imprecations against Romeo with ambiguous remarks that conceal her real feelings, she is caught short momentarily by Lady Capulet's information that she will marry Paris "early next Thursday morn" (3.5.112). She stoutly refuses, once more showing her independent spirit; but when her father enters, she is unable to deflect his anger, even beseeching him on her knees. She turns to her mother for support but finds none there either. Abandoned by both parents, she asks the Nurse for advice. The counsel Juliet receives so violates her moral sensibility that she knows she can never again depend on the Nurse for anything. "In a matter of seconds," Goddard says, "the child has become a woman" (*Meaning of Shakespeare,* p. 135), but impressive as the dramatic moment is—and it, too, is a kind of turning point, or pivot—Juliet's maturity has been steadily evolving despite, or rather through, the rapid sequence of events.[34]

One of her finest moments comes during her colloquy with Paris in Friar Lawrence's cell, where she has gone in desperation for help. Distraught though she may feel, her composure is absolute as she addresses the Count, who calmly and confidently greets her as his lady and his wife. In the stychomythia that follows, Juliet punctuates her replies with wit as well as dignity (4.1.18–36). After Paris leaves, her courage—her willingness to risk anything so that she may "live an unstained wife" (l. 88)—persuades the Friar to concoct a plan that just might work. Juliet jumps at the chance and reaches another dramatic climax when, after contemplating all the dangers involved in taking the Friar's potion, she drinks it off, pledging herself to Romeo as she does so.

Apart from its masterly rendering of "horror enacted in imagination," Juliet's soliloquy—as a soliloquy—underscores her growing and now-complete isolation. "What her imagination projects," Ruth Nevo continues, "is an image of the ultimate aloneness, the maximum distance which can be traveled by a human being from the sustaining and comforting presence of his kind."[35] That she is capable of carrying out her "dismal scene" alone is clear, for this is exactly what she does; but Shakespeare first lets us know how terrible her act appears. Final testimony to Juliet's courage and maturity comes when she awakens in the tomb from her trancelike state. Her first thought is for Romeo, as she addresses her "comfortable" Friar. But he proves to be something less than comfortable after all, pointing to the bodies of both Romeo and Paris and urging her to flee with him. She refuses. Once again, and for the last time, she shows her independent spirit and her integrity, expressed in devotion to her husband, whom she is determined to join in death. The cup emptied of poison and Romeo's lips providing no "restorative," she resorts to his dagger.

Compared with Romeo's suicide, Juliet's is much briefer, necessarily so in dramatic terms. But dramatic necessity aside, with her faith in the Friar shattered, her unquestioning choice of death makes a fitting end for her, as Granville-Barker says. "In the unreflecting haste of it all lies her peculiar tragedy," he concludes. "One day a child, and the next a woman!"[36] But as we have seen, her transformation has not been quite that sudden; her maturity has developed over the course of events, much as Romeo's has, though not quite in the same way. Whether he or she emerges as the principal protagonist is immaterial, as Shakespeare knew when he named his tragedy. Both are tragic figures, and both heroic.

NOTES

1. Franklin M. Dickey, *Not Wisely but Too Well* (San Marino: Huntington Library, 1957), pp. 66, 74. Cp. Maynard Mack, *Everybody's Shakespeare* (Lincoln: University of Nebraska Press, 1993), p. 69, and Rosalie L. Colie, *Shakespeare's Living Art* (Princeton, N.J.: Princeton University Press, 1974), p. 136.

2. See Colie, *Shakespeare's Living Art*, pp. 135–46, and cp. H. B. Charlton, *Shakespearian Tragedy* (Cambridge: Cambridge University Press, 1948), pp. 49–61.

3. On Juliet's relationships with her mother and father, see Irene G. Dash, *Wooing, Wedding, and Power: Women in Shakespeare's Plays* (New York: Columbia University Press, 1981), pp. 69–75, 90–92.

4. *As You Like It* 1.1.114–19. See Jay L. Halio, " 'No Clock in the Forest': Time in *As You Like It*," *SEL* (Studies in English Literature), 2 (1962): 197–207, for more on this subject and its relation to the representatives of a younger generation.

5. See Harley Granville-Barker, *Prefaces to Shakespeare*, 4 vols. (1930; rpt. London: Batsford, 1963), vol. 4, p. 80, on Capulet's inconsistencies and the distortions of his character in modern productions.

6. See, for example, G. B. Evans, ed., *New Cambridge Shakespeare* (Cambridge: Cambridge University Press, 1984), p. 24.

7. Ibid., pp. 23–24. Evans concludes: "Even the Friar, as spectator, would have violated the privacy of her union with Romeo and death." Cp. Dash, *Wooing*, p. 96, who considers the Friar directly responsible for Juliet's suicide, when "no restraining hand present and abandoned by the Friar, she believes herself without an alternative." Of course, the Friar has presented the alternative of disposing her "Among a sisterhood of holy nuns" (5.3.157), but Juliet instantly rejects his offer.

8. Harold Goddard, *The Meaning of Shakespeare* (Chicago: University of Chicago Press, 1951), p. 120. He compares the Nurse to the devil in a morality play. Cp. Granville-Barker, *Prefaces*, vol. 4, pp. 77–79.

9. Goddard, *Meaning of Shakespeare*, p. 121.

10. Mack, *Everybody's Shakespeare*, p. 83. Benvolio literally translates as "well wishing," as Jill Levenson glosses his name in her Oxford edition. Mercutio's jocular description of him as a "hot Jack" (3.1.5–26) can hardly be taken seriously; note Benvolio's astonishment in his replies.

11. In Q1, after Montague tells the Prince that his wife has died, he also mentions Benvolio's death, but gives no explanation for either one. In Q2, which is altogether silent concerning Benvolio, Montague says that grief over Romeo's banishment has caused his wife's death (5.3.210–11). Presumably, the actor who played Benvolio was needed for another role, perhaps the Captain of the Watch, and could not appear at the end; but whatever the reason, his dramatic function was by then finished, and Shakespeare could dispense with him.

12. Evans's gloss, *New Cambridge Shakespeare*. Cp. Mercutio's earlier disparagement of Tybalt, 2.4.18–31.

13. See Jerzy Limon, "Rehabilitating Tybalt: A New Interpretation of the Duel Scene in *Romeo and Juliet*," in *"Romeo and Juliet": Texts, Contexts, and Interpretation*, ed. Jay L. Halio (Newark: University of Delaware Press, 1995), pp. 97–106.

14. Cp. Joseph A. Porter, *Shakespeare's Mercutio* (Chapel Hill: University of North Carolina Press, 1988), p. 102. Porter compares Mercutio's role to that of Mercury advising Odysseus and Aeneas to end their infatuations and notes that while Mercutio is essentially active, Romeo is reactive or passive when he is with him (p. 103).

15. Mack, *Everybody's Shakespeare*, p. 77.

16. Cp. Colie, *Shakespeare's Living Art*, p. 141: "Mercutio provides . . . an Ovidian voice, that of the high-spirited libertine whose awareness of the physical delights of love balances the sweetness, the near nambypambyness of the Petrarchan traditional language" that Romeo and Juliet use early in the play. In a sense, Edward Snow argues, Mercutio has to die before Romeo and Juliet's relationship can be sexually consummated, or so the plot seems to tell us; see "Language and Sexual Difference in *Romeo and Juliet*," in *Shakespeare's "Rough Magic,"* ed. Peter Erickson and Coppélia Kahn (Newark: University of Delaware Press, 1985), p. 186.

17. This is Samuel Coleridge's observation; see *Coleridge's Shakespearean Criticism,* ed. T. M. Raysor, 2 vols. (London: Constable, 1930), vol. 2, pp. 118–19.

18. Goddard, *Meaning of Shakespeare,* pp. 122–24. Cp. Robert O. Evans, *The Osier Cage* (Lexington: University of Kentucky Press, 1966), pp. 68–86. Evans argues that the speech is only an apparent digression but has an important dramatic function in the wit combat carried on with Romeo immediately prior (pp. 72–76). He also defends the speech as thematically significant (pp. 78–80). For another extended analysis of the Queen Mab speech as it relates to dream theory and Mercutio's verbal wit, see Marjorie Garber, *Dream in Shakespeare* (New Haven, Conn.: Yale University Press, 1974), pp. 37–42.

19. For Shakespeare's descriptions of the distraught lover, see *As You Like It* 3.2.370–81 and *Hamlet* 2.1.74–80. Romeo may not look quite like Ophelia's description of Hamlet, or Rosalind's of the typical lover, but he sounds enough like lovesick Orlando.

20. See Limon, "Rehabilitating Tybalt," p. 101.

21. Granville-Barker, *Prefaces,* vol. 4, p. 89.

22. This is the Q1 stage direction, which most modern editors adopt.

23. Hamlet is absent after 4.4 until the beginning of act 5, when he reenters Denmark, appropriately and symbolically, through the graveyard where Ophelia will be buried. Then and in the following scene, 5.2, he seems calmer and more resigned to his destiny—to his role as Heaven's "scourge and minister"—despite his outburst to Laertes. Richard leaves

England to fight in Ireland after 2.2 and does not return until 3.2, when he appears a much more noble and sympathetic figure than he did in the first half of the play.

24. Cp. Irving Ribner, *Patterns in Shakesperian Tragedy* (New York: Barnes and Noble, 1960), pp. 32–33. Ribner prefers the Q2 reading, "denie you starres," and sees Romeo asserting here his independence of fortune.

25. Cp. Ruth Nevo, *Tragic Form in Shakespeare* (Princeton, N.J.: Princeton University Press, 1972), p. 53: "[Romeo's] self-control contrasts with his self-abandonment in the Friar's cell when told of his banishment, but, by a paradox which is only apparent, is the measure of his loss of all hope. His darkened vision of the world which he now repudiates is given remarkable 'objective correlative' in the episode of the meager apothecary."

26. Cp. Brian Gibbons, New Arden edition (London: Methuen, 1980), p. 50: "By the beginning of the last scene, Romeo's transformation of personality is expressed in a new note of resolution and command, compressed resonant and personal." See also Douglas Cole, "Introduction," *Twentieth Century Interpretations of "Romeo and Juliet,"* ed. Douglas Cole (Englewood Cliffs, N.J.: Prentice-Hall, 1970), p. 13.

27. See, for example, Dash, *Wooing*, pp. 68–73. Whether Shakespeare actually changed her age from Brooke's "xvi. yeres" or simply misread the numeral—or whether he read an edition that transposed the last two digits, as the nineteenth-century editor Richard Grant White suggested—is uncertain. Cp. Granville-Barker, *Prefaces*, vol. 4, p. 92 n, who notes that Shakespeare may have reduced Juliet's age to suit the very youthful appearance of some boy actress; in any case, fourteen is not distinguishable from sixteen on the stage. But Robert O. Evans argues in *The Osier Cage*, p. 31, that Shakespeare must have deliberately altered Juliet's age because he "needed a young girl just on the threshold of sexual awakening . . . who could not possibly have had any previous romantic experiences." Cp. also Peter Laslett's discussion of marital ages in *The World We Have Lost Further Explored,* 3rd ed. (London: Methuen, 1983).

28. Mack, *Everybody's Shakespeare*, p. 84.

29. Cp. *The Tempest* 3.1.81–90, where Miranda asks Ferdinand if he will be her husband. Married love is a recurrent theme in Shakespeare.

30. It is only a few hours in chronological time, but in dramatic terms, much longer, given the events of 3.1. On Shakespeare's handling of time, see Granville-Barker, *Prefaces,* vol. 4, pp. 44, 100–102, and cp. Halio, " 'No Clock in the Forest.' "

31. See *Antony and Cleopatra* 5.1.79–92.

32. Gibbons, New Arden edition, p. 170. Most recent editions retain the Q/F reading "I" at line 21, rather than the Q4 emendation "he" adopted by earlier editors. For an analysis that fully justifies the Q/F reading, see Snow, "Language and Sexual Difference," pp. 189–90 n. 5: in the Q/F reading, Juliet "takes" Romeo with her in her "death." Snow notes the analogy in the final scene, where again Juliet uses "die" ambiguously in this way. Cp. Nicholas Brooke, *Shakespeare's Early Tragedies* (London: Methuen, 1968), p. 101: "Juliet's speech is itself magnificently alive, but it leaps straight into death."

33. For example, Dash, *Wooing*, pp. 96–98. Cp. Goddard, *Meaning of Shakespeare,* pp. 135–36, and Evans, *The Osier Cage,* pp. 34–39.

34. Cp. Snow, "Language and Sexual Difference," p. 183, who notes that the rupture is completed later when the Nurse fails to waken Juliet in 4.5.

35. Nevo, *Tragic Form,* p. 53.

36. Granville-Barker, *Prefaces,* vol. 4, p. 98.

5

LANGUAGE

In the plays written before *Romeo and Juliet*, Shakespeare had already feasted on the banquets the English language afforded, especially in *Love's Labour's Lost* (1595), but his appetite (to paraphrase Enobarbus on Cleopatra's effect) seemed to grow by what it fed on. Throughout his career, as many commentators have remarked, he constantly pushed the resources of his primary medium—words—to their utmost boundary, both in verse and in prose. *Romeo and Juliet* is one of the best examples of how he adapted English drama to the love poetry of his time and place, particularly the kind of poetry he had already developed and continued to develop in his long erotic narrative poems, *Venus and Adonis* (1593) and *The Rape of Lucrece* (1594), and in his sequence of sonnets, which circulated among his friends but was not published until 1609.

VERSE

As if to prepare his audience for part of what was to come, Shakespeare began *Romeo and Juliet* with a sonnet-speaking Chorus, or Prologue, using the form he had also used for his sonnet sequence, rather than the Italian form Petrarch used; that is, three quatrains followed by a couplet, instead of an octet rhyming *abba abba,* followed by a sestet.[1] Petrarch, however, is otherwise much in evidence, especially in the first half of the play. Romeo's infatuation with Rosaline inspires the purest Petrarch, moving Mercutio to salute him with "Now is he for the numbers that Petrarch flowed in" (2.4.34). Although by then the taunt is no longer relevant, Mercutio does not know this; he is reacting to the Romeo who, in his first dialogue with Benvolio, unabashedly apes the Petrarchan "numbers." His lines there typify the conventional lover's versifying, complaining of the treatment by his Cruel Mistress:

> she'll not be hit
> With Cupid's arrow, she hath Dian's wit;
> And in strong proof of chastity well armed,
> From Love's weak childish bow she lives uncharmed.
> She will not stay the siege of loving terms,
> Nor bide th'encounter of assailing eyes,
> Nor ope her lap to saint-seducing gold.
> O, she is rich in beauty, only poor
> That when she dies, with beauty dies her store. (1.1.199–207)

The last couplet reprises a theme Shakespeare uses in Sonnets 3, 4, and 11, but the preceding lines, mostly in rhyme, restate in familiar terms the lover's familiar lament. Romeo's clichés play upon the Epicurean argument for love, using the carpe diem ("seize the day") theme reminiscent of many love lyrics from the ancients to their Renaissance imitators.[2]

Romeo is not alone in his use of conventional language, although his idiom changes as the object of his devotion changes. When Lady Capulet, for example, attempts to interest Juliet in the County Paris early in the play, she describes him in copybook terms:

> Read o'er the volume of young Paris' face,
> And find delight writ there with beauty's pen;
> Examine every married lineament,
> And see how one another lends content;
> And what obscured in this fair volume lies,
> Find written in the margent of his eyes. (1.3.82–87)

Lady Capulet's conceit, or extended metaphor, continues for several more lines, illustrative of a self-indulgent tendency attributable perhaps to the author—who in this play and others of the lyrical group is given to such indulgences—but in this instance he may be using such language to bring out a character trait in Juliet's conventionally minded mother.[3] Even Juliet sometimes falls into conventionality and stereotype, as when she first hears that Romeo has killed her cousin Tybalt. Her series of oxymora may be compared with Romeo's in 1.1.167–73; they express her "crisis of doubt," but like Romeo's in their evident artificiality, they sound unconvincing.[4] The use of clichés *as* clichés is more characteristic of the speech of the older generation, for example, in Montague's references to "The shady curtains of Aurora's bed" (1.1.127) and to the "envious worm" destroying a bud before it can "spread his sweet leaves to the air" (1.1.142–43).[5]

When Romeo and Juliet meet, the sonnet form reappears, with its "extra" quatrain (1.5.92–107). One commentator has described the studied formality as "a marvelous sublimation of the witty exchange of young people meeting and trying each other out."[6] Another notices how the couple's first words to each other, dividing a sonnet between them, presses "a powerful seal, as it were, upon their meeting, at once linking themselves together with an invisible bond."[7] The language of "pilgrims" and "saints" is the language of contemporary sonneteers, minor poets whom Shakespeare elsewhere satirized. But not here. Romeo and Juliet speak the fashionable love language of their time, at least at first; if they are "playing like minor poets within the current mode,"[8] they do so with purpose, fully conscious of what they are about. After all, this is only the beginning of their relationship; fuller and deeper expressions of love come later.

They come, first, in the balcony, or garden, scene after both have learned that they are members of the opposing families, whose bloody rivalry the play has already dramatized. Although vestiges of the sonnet language persist here and later, as in Romeo's apostrophe to Juliet's eyes (2.2.15–22) and in Juliet's use of snow imagery upon a raven's back (3.2.18–19),[9] the direction their language takes is to greater simplicity and directness.[10] Here, for example, is how they begin speaking to each other after Romeo has revealed himself to Juliet:

> JULIET   What man art thou that thus bescreened in night
> So stumblest on my counsel?
>
> ROMEO   By a name
> I know not how to tell thee who I am.
> My name, dear saint, is hateful to myself,
> Because it is an enemy to thee;
> Had I it written, I would tear the word. (2.2.51–56)

In entirely unvarnished terms Juliet conveys her anxiety that Romeo may be discovered: "If they do see thee, they will murder thee"; "I would not for the world they saw thee here"; and then, reassured, she allows her curiosity to speak: "By whose direction found'st thou out this place?" (ll. 70, 74, 79). Romeo again reverts to sonnet language (ll. 80–84), but not Juliet. She might have played coy, she says, "but farewell compliment"; and she gets right to the point: "Dost thou love me?" (l. 90). Before he can answer, she continues:

> But trust me, gentleman, I'll prove more true
> Than those that have more coying to be strange. (ll. 101–2)

When Romeo tries to swear how much he loves her, she cuts him off repeatedly, doubtless recognizing the artificiality of his lover's vows; she ends by telling him not to swear at all. Like Shakespeare's other heroines, her sense of practical reality breaks through:

> Well, do not swear. Although I joy in thee,
> I have no joy of this contract tonight,
> It is too rash, too unadvised, too sudden,
> Too like lightning, which doth cease to be
> Ere one can say 'It lightens.' (ll. 116–20)

But her love is already too strong to let her leave things quite like that. Their leave-taking, in fact, goes on for another seventy lines, punctuated by the intrusions of the Nurse's calls, the voice of another reality. Exchanging vows, Juliet says in all ingenuousness:

> My bounty is as boundless as the sea,
> My love as deep; the more I give to thee
> The more I have, for both are infinite. (ll. 133–35)

Still unwilling to break off their colloquy, Juliet returns yet another time, after Romeo has begun to leave. Her language now is both earthy and allusive:

> Hist, Romeo, hist! O for a falc'ner's voice,
> To lure that tassel-gentle back again:
> Bondage is hoarse, and may not speak aloud,
> Else would I tear the cave where Echo lies,
> And make her airy tongue more hoarse than mine
> With repetition of my Romeo's name. (ll. 158–63)

By her language and her actions Juliet has taken control of this scene.[11] Romeo, for his part, is wonderstruck:

> O blessèd, blessèd night! I am afeard,
> Being in night, all this is but a dream,
> Too flattering-sweet to be substantial. (ll. 139–41)

But though it is night, it is no dream. Juliet's reality and the reality of her love for Romeo are both pronounced and definite.[12]

Their love poetry pervades the play and more than anything else gives it its outstanding quality. To cite one other exquisite example: the aubade in act 3. A poem in the courtly love tradition, the aubade is a dawn song after a night of love, but Shakespeare here gives the poem "a sharper edge."[13] In the courtly love poem, the man leaves at dawn because secrecy is part of the code, but Romeo has more pressing reasons: his life is at risk unless he leaves Verona by daybreak. Moreover, the couple are married lovers, which gives the familiar argument over which bird sang, the lark or the nightingale, its "peculiar poignancy and relevance."[14]

> JULIET   Wilt thou be gone? It is not yet near day:
>   It was the nightingale, not the lark,
>   That pierced the fearful hollow of thine ear;
>   Nightly she sings on yond pomegranate tree.
>   Believe me, love, it was the nightingale.
>
> ROMEO   It was the lark, the herald of the morn,
>   No nightingale. Look, love, what envious streaks
>   Do lace the severing clouds in yonder east:

> Night's candles are burnt out, and jocund day
> Stands tiptoe on the misty mountain tops.
> I must be gone and live, or stay and die. (3.5.1–11)

After a few more lines of this, Romeo yields, but his capitulation brings Juliet back to earth, as she, too, realizes the danger he is in. She admits that "It is the lark that sings so out of tune, / Straining harsh discords and unpleasing sharps" and cries, "O now be gone, more light and light it grows" (ll. 27–28, 35). Romeo's response epitomizes the paradox of their situation: "More light and light, more dark and dark our woes!"

Along with the sonnet and aubade, Shakespeare uses many other forms of poetry in this play, sometimes called "set pieces" or—using a musical analogy—arias, such as Juliet's epithalamium (3.2.1–31), Mercutio's rhapsody on Queen Mab (1.4.53–95), Friar Lawrence's sermons and sententiae (3.3.108–45), Paris's elegy (5.3.11–17), and so forth. Although blank verse predominates, rhymed iambic pentameter couplets are also much in evidence, especially in the first half of the play. According to Ralph Berry, rhyme is "the shared possession" of Veronese society. "The Veronese think in rhyme, and communicate in rhyme," he says,[15] citing Friar Lawrence's soliloquy in 2.3, which does not change either in meter or in tone after Romeo's arrival; in fact, Romeo responds in exactly the same mode. Their dialogue develops a kind of ritual or liturgical quality as a result. Berry goes on to differentiate between two varieties of rhyme used elsewhere in the play: (1) the "heavy, jogging rhymes" of the elders, which have a self-fulfilling prophecy, or inevitability, about them ("night" *must* follow "light," etc.); and (2) the quicker, more versatile rhyme of the younger people, which picks up the loose ends of a companion's speech, for instance, when Romeo rhymes Benvolio's "thy good heart's oppression" with "love's transgression" (1.1.175–76).

Nevertheless, blank verse is the chief medium for this drama, as for Shakespeare's later tragedies, where it is used almost exclusively except in songs or at the end of scenes.[16] *Romeo and Juliet,* however, presents some surprises. Just as in *The Tempest* Shakespeare has Caliban, an unlikely character, speak in blank verse, so here the Nurse also speaks in blank verse where, given her nature and her social station, we might otherwise expect prose. It may be an accident of circumstance, as G. R. Hibbard suggests, that makes the Nurse's first speeches occur in verse, for she is in the company of Lady Capulet and Juliet, who speak in blank verse, and Shakespeare may have felt it necessary to continue the scene in that mode.[17] But that would be to deny the playwright complete control, and he is by no means averse to mixing verse and prose in similar situations elsewhere.[18] More to the point, Shakespeare endows the Nurse with a kind of blank verse that is uniquely hers, blank verse that has an extraordinary flexibility and range, inelegant though it may be. The end-stopped lines notwithstanding, her verses capture the rhythms and tones of colloquial speech—something new in dramatic blank verse, which heretofore was more formalized and regular.[19]

> Even or odd, of all days of the year,
> Come Lammas-eve at night she shall be fourteen.
> Susan and she—God rest all Christian souls!—
> Were of an age. Well, Susan is with God,
> She was too good for me. But as I said . . . . (1.3.17–21)

And so she goes on, intermingling remembered dialogue, stories, bawdry in a steady stream of talk—good, earthy talk—never before heard in blank verse, though it may somewhat derive from the rhymed verse of earlier drama, which was part of Shakespeare's heritage.[20] Later, during the ball, Shakespeare further experiments with colloquial language in blank verse, using it for the conversation between Capulet and his cousin (1.5.29–39). Their dialogue, couched in the "homeliest russet and kersey" speech, serves no obvious dramatic function, except possibly to contrast with and thus highlight Romeo's more elegant language when he asks a servingman, "What lady's that which doth enrich the hand / Of yonder knight?" and then breaks into his elaborate apostrophe to Juliet's beauty (ll. 40–52).[21]

PROSE

Shakespeare's prose matches the flexibility and versatility of Shakespeare's verse, as well as its variousness. Or, to put it another way, "the poetry and prose of this play complement each other exquisitely."[22] The lofty poetry of the lovers is balanced—one might even say anchored—by the simple diction of the servants, who speak a colorful, rhythmic prose, for instance, at the beginning of the ball scene in 1.5. Just as Peter Quince and his fellows in *A Midsummer Night's Dream* transport us effortlessly from Athens to Warwickshire and back again, so these servingmen in their eagerness to prepare and serve the feast convey a homely familiarity and worldly wisdom:

> FIRST SERVINGMAN   Where's Potpan, that he helps not to take away? He shift a trencher? he scrape a trencher?
>
> SECOND SERVINGMAN   When good manners shall lie all in one or two men's hands, and they unwashed too, 'tis a foul thing.
>
> FIRST SERVINGMAN   Away with the join-stools, remove the court-cupboard, look to the plate. Good thou, save me a piece of marchpane, and as thou loves me, let the porter let in Susan Grindstone and Nell. (1.5.1–8)

These and a few more lines serve as preface to the blank verse of Old Capulet's welcome to his guests, the music playing, Capulet's reminiscences with his cousin, and the first high point of the scene: Romeo's initial sight of Juliet (1.5.43–52). The passage contrasts with the scurrilous dialogue between Sampson and Gregory that opens the play and leads to the violent conflict between Capulets and Montagues, just as the low wit and humor there contrast with the witty dialogue of Romeo and Mercutio.

Mercutio, who speaks in verse as well as prose, rivals Falstaff in his verbal facility. As Milton Crane remarks, his prose is "a constant delight, ever in motion, shifting its ground, suddenly parrying and thrusting."[23] If he is what Romeo was before he fell for Rosaline, as Crane suggests, he soon brings Romeo back to his old self, if not in 1.4 (a verse scene), then in 2.4 in prose. He flings a teasing greeting at his friend:

> O flesh, flesh, how art thou fishified. Now is he for the numbers Petrarch flowed in. Laura to his lady was a kitchen wench (marry, she had a better love to berhyme her), Dido a dowdy, Cleopatra a gipsy, Helen and Hero hildings and harlots, Thisbe a grey eye or so, but not to the purpose. Signior Romeo, 'bon jour'! (2.4.33–38)

And so on. Romeo takes a moment to get his bearings and then joins in, matching Mercutio gibe for gibe until his friend feigns a swoon:

> MERCUTIO   Sure wit! Follow me this jest now, till thou hast worn out thy pump, that when the single sole of it is worn, the jest may remain, after the wearing, solely singular.
>
> ROMEO   O single-soled jest, solely singular for the singleness!
>
> MERCUTIO   Come between us, good Benvolio, my wits faints. (ll. 53–57)

They go on, until Mercutio asks rhetorically, "Why, is this not better now than groaning for love? Now art thou sociable, now art thou Romeo; now art thou what thou art, by art as well as nature" (ll. 72–74), and his talk turns bawdy. At this point Benvolio takes over and continues the scabrous wit sallies, until the Nurse enters with her man Peter and Mercutio finds a different target.

The Nurse, however, talker that she is, is no match for Mercutio, who, recognizing this (ll. 103–4), goes off improvising a bawdy song directed at her. Where Mercutio's prose was witty and agile, the Nurse's is cumbersome and confused, filled with repetitions and false starts, as befits her character, for example, in this speech to Romeo after Mercutio leaves:

> Now afore God, I am so vexed that every part about me quivers. Scurvy knave! Pray you sir, a word: and as I told you, my young lady bid me enquire you out; what she bid me say, I will keep to myself. But first let me tell ye, if ye should lead her in a fool's paradise, as they say, it were a very gross kind of behaviour, as they say; for the gentlewoman is young; and therefore, if you should deal double with her, truly it were an ill thing to be offered to any gentlewoman, and very weak dealing. (ll. 133–40)

This is the very antithesis to the scintillating prose of Mercutio, Romeo, and Benvolio, with which it obviously contrasts. So does its humor, which is of a low order by comparison. But it is consistent with the verse she speaks elsewhere, again testimony to Shakespeare's ability to employ one mode or another as occasion warrants or as he sees fit.

And, strange though it may seem at first, he sees fit to end the scene of Juliet's supposed death and her family's mourning with the prose of Peter and the musicians (4.5.96–138). Why? Crane suggests that Will Kemp, who played Peter and was the then most famous clown on the Elizabethan stage, may have demanded a longer part.[24] That well might be true, but it is insufficient dramatic justification for the mixture of tragedy and low comedy at this moment. Shakespeare may have inserted it to reassure the audience of the possible happy outcome, if the Friar's plan works; for, as we know, Juliet is not really dead. Whatever the case, the musicians, whom Paris has sent to escort his bride to the wedding, recognize how the situation has changed and begin to put up their instruments. Then Peter enters and demands that they play "Heart's ease," that is, "some merry dump to comfort me." The musicians refuse, commenting that it is "no time to play now," but Peter insists. In the ensuing contretemps, Peter becomes more and more obstreperous and threatening. He begins singing himself and questions the musicians on the meaning of some of the words. He calls the musicians by their proper names, which just happen to be the names, too, of the instruments they play, or certain parts of them: Simon Catling, Hugh Rebeck, James Soundpost. We are not far from—indeed Shakespeare anticipates—the "rude mechanicals" and their behavior in *A Midsummer Night's Dream,* whose names also reflect their occupations.[25]

To return to Mercutio's prose, which reaches its high point and its culmination in 3.1: Although Benvolio begins the scene in verse, Mercutio responds in resounding prose, berating his companion with a description more appropriate to Tybalt, who soon enters, or to himself than it is to Benvolio. He uses vivid images from the ordinary life of a gentleman, rhythmically compelling cadences, and familiar but not low terms, as in these lines:

> Thy head is as full of quarrels as an egg is full of meat, and yet thy head hath been beaten as addle as an egg for quarreling. Thou hast quarrelled with a man for coughing in the street, because he hath wakened thy dog that hath lain asleep in the sun. Didst thou fall out with a tailor for wearing his new doublet before Easter? with another for wearing his new shoes with old riband? and yet thou wilt tutor me for quarrelling? (ll. 19–26)

It is a tour de force, entertaining in itself, as it is supposed to be, but also a prelude to what follows. For when Tybalt civilly approaches them, he gets anything but a civil reply—from Mercutio, who takes every opportunity to antagonize him. Mercutio has earlier expressed his disdain for Tybalt (2.4.18–31), so we are somewhat prepared for this exchange, but not for what happens after Romeo enters.

Tybalt and Romeo speak in blank verse, as befits their formal discourse, but Mercutio cannot abide it. After three lines of verse, he resorts to vigorous prose to challenge Tybalt and avenge his friend's "calm, dishonourable, vile submission" (ll. 66–74). When he is wounded, he again starts speaking in verse and reverts to prose, using the same idiom as before. The "impatient brevity" and "mocking repetitions" that he had used in satirizing Tybalt in 2.4 reappear in " 'Zounds, a dog, a rat, a mouse, a cat, to scratch a man to death! a braggart, a rogue, a villain, that fights by the book of arithmetic" (ll. 91–93).[26] He dies, as he lived, with a jest. Describing his wound, he says:

> No, 'tis not so deep as a well, nor so wide as a church-door, but 'tis enough, 'twill serve. Ask for me tomorrow, and you shall find me a grave man. (ll. 88–90)

IMAGERY

Shakespeare thought in images, and the patterns of imagery in his plays are often a key to the themes he develops. They are also a key to the way he perceived his characters and wanted his audience to see them. Caroline Spurgeon, a pioneer in the study of Shakespeare's imagery, notes how Romeo and Juliet each thinks of the other as light, which becomes the dominating image in the play.[27] Romeo conveys his "overpowering impression" when he first sees Juliet:

> O she doth teach the torches to burn bright!
> It seems she hangs upon the cheek of night
> As a rich jewel in an Ethiop's ear—(1.5.42–45)

Likewise, to Juliet, Romeo is "day in night," who lies upon the night "Whiter than new snow upon a raven's back" (3.2.17–19). Their passionate intensity informs even the most tired imagery with new energy, as in Romeo's comparisons of Juliet's eyes to stars (2.2.15–22) or Juliet's similar conceit (3.2.21–25). The imagery continues to the very end: Romeo sees Juliet's tomb not as a grave, but as a lantern, for her "beauty makes / This vault a feasting presence full of light" (5.3.85–86).

Not only images of the sun and stars, but those of lightning, fire, meteors, and the flash of gunpowder brighten and enliven the dialogue. Along with the compressed time frame, they led Spurgeon to believe that "Shakespeare saw the story, in its swift and tragic beauty, as an almost blinding flash of light, suddenly ignited, and as swiftly quenched" (*Shakespeare's Imagery,* p. 312). That may be, though we can never certainly know. Shakespeare used other images, more or less related to these dominant ones and more or less complex.[28] Romeo's depiction of Juliet in the balcony scene as a "bright angel" is new in the way it springs from the situation and the character who speaks:

> O speak again, bright angel, for thou art
> As glorious to this night, being o'er my head,
> As is a wingèd messenger of heaven
> Unto the white-upturnèd wond'ring eyes

> Of mortals that fall back to gaze on him,
> When he bestrides the lazy puffing clouds,
> And sails upon the bosom of the air. (2.2.26–32)

Wolfgang Clemen claims that "the situation is itself of such a metaphorical nature, that it permits an organic growth of the image" (*Development,* p. 67), as indeed it does. Romeo stands below in the garden and looks up at Juliet—and at the clouds moving in the dark sky above her. He imagines Juliet as a winged angel attracting the gaze of onlookers, like himself, whose "white-upturnéd eyes" are filled with awe at the wondrous sight they behold. According to Clemen, "everything in this image has a double function: the clouds and the heavenly *messengers* may be reality, and at the same time they are symbols" (ibid.). Moreover, the imagery and the moment inspire Romeo to rise above the levels of speech he had been capable of earlier. Three usually separate functions of imagery here merge: the image provides an enhanced expression of Romeo's nature, it characterizes Juliet, and it creates the atmosphere for the rest of the scene.[29]

The transmission of atmosphere is itself an important function of imagery in Elizabethan plays, usually performed in daylight with minimal scenery. In *Romeo and Juliet* Shakespeare learned how to do this while at the same time producing a closer harmony between the imagery and the characters, between the inner and the outer situation and the theme of the play.[30] A good example occurs in Juliet's epithalamium:

> Gallop apace you fiery-footed steeds,
> Toward Phoebus' lodging; such a waggoner
> As Phaëton would whip you to the west,
> And bring in cloudy night immediately.
> Spread thy close curtain, love-performing Night,
> That runaways' eyes may wink, and Romeo
> Leap to these arms, untalked of and unseen. (3.2.1–7)

Juliet's invocation to night is both dramatically motivated and a function of her character, not something added or tacked on to the dialogue to indicate approaching darkness. During the ball scene, Shakespeare uses a similar technique to suggest a crowded ambience in a dim hall grown too warm by the excitement and dancing, when Old Capulet commands his servants:

> Come, musicians, play.
>
> *Music plays.*
>
> A hall, a hall, give room! and foot it, girls.
>
> *And they dance.*
>
> More light, you knaves, and turn the tables up;
> And quench the fire, the room is grown too hot. (1.5.23–26)

Before the ball, Mercutio and Romeo (who bears a torch) play on the literal and figurative senses of "daylight" while indicating that it is night:

MERCUTIO   Come, we burn daylight, ho!

ROMEO   Nay, that's not so.

MERCUTIO   I mean, sir, in delay
We waste our lights in vain, like lights by day. (1.4.43–45)

The aubade in 3.5. is another example of speeches dramatically motivated that also fuse nature and nature images. When Paris, in the last scene, orders his page to hold his ear close to the ground under yew trees, he says the churchyard is "loose, unfirm with digging up of graves" (5.3.6), thereby describing the landscape and preparing for Friar Lawrence's entrance later on: "St. Francis be my speed! how oft tonight / Have my old feet stumbled at graves!" (ll. 121–22). The Prince's closing lines may be guilty of a pathetic fallacy, but they none the less convey the proper atmosphere for the day that dawns: "A glooming peace this morning with it brings, / The sun for sorrow will not show its face" (ll. 305–6).

The most spectacular imagery in *Romeo and Juliet* undoubtedly occurs in Mercutio's Queen Mab speech (1.4.53–95). Often regarded as an "interlude" or digression,[31] it seems to serve no dramatic purpose. Although some critics have sprung to its defense,[32] and no dramatic performance would dare omit it altogether, it remains a set speech, calling attention to itself and its speaker, but not moving the action of the play forward. On the other hand, the speech in itself is hardly static; it moves onward at a pace far quicker than the verse that surrounds it.[33] Rapidly mounting concrete, minute details, which provide a vivid, moving picture of Queen Mab and her coach, Mercutio's lines also convey a sense of childlike wonder. For the moment, at least, they endear us to him and to his fantasy—until he mocks her.[34] At first "the fairies' midwife" (l. 54), Mab ends up a "hag" (l. 92), no longer engendering wishful dreams (ll. 70–81), but engaging in mischief, plaiting the manes of horses at night—or worse (ll. 89–94).[35] Romeo has to interrupt to stop Mercutio, and indeed he has gone on long enough. At this, his idiom changes with his tenor:

> True, I talk of dreams,
> Which are the children of an idle brain,
> Begot of nothing but vain fantasy,
> Which is as thin of substance as the air,
> And more inconstant than the wind, who woos
> Even now the frozen bosom of the north,
> And being angered puffs away from thence,
> Turning his side to the dew-dropping south. (ll. 96–103)

We are back to atmospherics and personifications, requiring Benvolio, playing on the figurative sense of wind, to bring his friends back to practical reality: "This wind you talk of blows us from ourselves: / Supper is done, and we shall come too late" (ll. 104–5). Romeo also quips, but in a more somber vein, voicing his presentiments of disaster: "I fear too early, for my mind misgives / Some consequence yet hanging in the stars."

WORDPLAY

A pun, said Samuel Johnson, not altogether missing the point, was Shakespeare's "fatal Cleopatra for which he lost the world and was content to lose it."[36] Johnson, of course, reflects the taste and attitude of his neoclassical age, which scorned what was regarded as a low form of wit in favor of "correctness" and *le mot juste*. And yet, as his editorial glosses show, Johnson often could appreciate Shakespeare's use of the "uncomic" pun, one that exploits the rich ambiguities of experience language helps to convey. In *Romeo and Juliet,* Shakespeare employed many varieties of wordplay, from the low puns and quibbles Gregory and Sampson enjoy using in the opening scene, to the more powerful ones such as Mercutio's when, dying, he says, "Ask for me tomorrow, and you shall find me a grave man" (3.1.89–90).

Puns and quibbles abound in *Romeo and Juliet*. By M. M. Mahood's conservative estimate, there are 175 of them. How they function is of more importance, however; they not only afford the characters an outlet for their often complex or contradictory feelings, as in Juliet's dialogue with her mother in 3.5.80–123, they also sharpen the play's dramatic irony. When Juliet sends the Nurse to ask Romeo's name, she says: "If he be marrièd, / My grave is like to be my wedding bed" (1.5.133–34). The irony here is that, while Romeo in fact is not married, their wedding leads directly to the deaths of both of them, although neither they nor the audience knows this, despite the characters' various forebodings.[37] (The wordplay lies in recognizing the grave as a bed.) The wordplay continues when Juliet learns that "yond gentleman" is Romeo and a Montague: "My only love sprung from my only hate!" (l. 137). If Mahood is right, wordplay in *Romeo and Juliet* "clarifies the conflict of incompatible truths and helps to establish their final equipoise" (*Shakespeare's Wordplay,* p. 56).

Much of the humor in the play also derives from ambiguities, particularly bawdy jokes that depend upon a more or less veiled secondary or tertiary meaning. Sampson and Gregory's puns (1.1.1–30) are too obvious to require comment, and some of Mercutio's jokes are not much above their level. For example, when he fails to find Romeo after the ball scene, Mercutio expresses his frustration in a series of bawdy double entendres:

> Now will he sit under a medlar tree,
> And wish his mistress were that kind of fruit
> As maids call medlars, when they laugh alone.

O Romeo, that she were, O that she were
An open *et cetera*,[38] thou a pop'rin pear! (2.1.34–38)

But Mercutio's wordplay is usually of a more sophisticated sort, especially when he crosses verbal swords with Romeo, as in 2.4 (see above) or with Tybalt in 3.1. Tybalt's comment, "Mercutio, thou consortest with Romeo," evokes this rejoinder:

> Consort? what, does thou make us minstrels? And thou make minstrels of us, look to hear nothing but discords. Here's my fiddlestick, here's that shall make you dance. (ll. 39–42)

The Nurse's puns are sometimes deliberate and sometimes not, as in the passage below, but almost invariably bawdy:

> And 'a speak anything against me, I'll take him down, and 'a were lustier than he is, and twenty such Jacks; and if I cannot, I'll find those that shall. Scurvy knave, I am none of his flirt-gills, I am none of his skains-mates. [*She turns to Peter, her man.*] And thou must stand by too and suffer every knave to use me at his pleasure! (2.4.125–29)

Peter at once picks up the ambiguity and plays on it:

> I saw no man use you at his pleasure; if I had, my weapon should quickly have been out. (ll. 130–31)[39]

Shakespeare's bawdry, however funny in itself—and *Romeo and Juliet* is one of his bawdiest plays—usually has a dramatic purpose.[40] Sampson and Gregory's quibbles, expressing a "brutal male dominance," as Mahood says (*Shakespeare's Wordplay,* p. 60), define one type of sexual relationship; Romeo's entrance later in 1.1, flowing in "Petrarch's numbers," expresses the opposite: man's subjection to woman's tyranny. Again, Mercutio's bawdry in 2.2 contrasts strikingly with the love poetry in the balcony scene that follows immediately and is joined to it by a shared couplet (2.1.42–2.2.1). The two aspects of love, physical and spiritual, opposed in these contexts, fuse after Romeo and Juliet are married.[41] A comic hint of this fusion occurs in the garden scene when the lovers begin their good-nights and Romeo complains: "O wilt thou leave me so unsatisfied?" Juliet replies, half in horror: "What satisfaction canst thou have tonight?" But Romeo reassures her that it is only the exchange of her "faithful vow" for his that he wants, and their colloquy briefly resumes, or rather intensifies, with Juliet's pledge of her "boundless" love (2.2.125–35).

As Sigmund Freud long ago noticed, stress can lead persons to express themselves in witty puns and quibbles. In Shakespeare's plays, some of the most unlikely characters[42] testify to this phenomenon; therefore, Juliet's playing on

I/ay/eye in her anxiety at 3.2 is psychologically sound, however else it may strike a modern audience:

> Hath Romeo slain himself? Say thou but 'ay',
> And that bare vowel 'I' shall poison more
> Than the death-darting eye of cockatrice.
> I am not I, if there be such an 'ay',
> Or those eyes shut, that makes thee answer 'ay'.
> If he be slain, say 'ay' or if not, 'no':
> Brief sounds determine my weal or woe. (ll. 45–51)

Similarly, stress occasions Romeo's obsessive repetitions of "banished" in 3.3, as well as his conceits and his pun on *flies/fly* (l. 41). His character, like his mood, has changed by the last scene; so has his use of ambiguity. In beckoning his lips to "seal with a righteous kiss / A dateless bargain to engrossing Death" (5.3.114–15), he develops a legal image (sealing), from which "bargain" follows and then "engrossing" in several senses: (1) purchasing in large quantities; (2) writing a legal document; and (3) illegally monopolizing or amassing.[43] His final lines convey his final ambiguity:

> Here's to my love! [*Drinks.*] O true apothecary!
> Thy drugs are quick. Thus with a kiss I die.

Mahood's commentary is apt:

> Like the Friar's herbs, the apothecary's poison both heals and destroys. He is *true* not only because he has spoken the truth to Romeo in describing the poison's potency, but because he has been true to his calling in finding a salve for Romeo's ills. His drugs are not only speedy, but also *quick* in the sense of "life-giving." Romeo and Juliet "cease to die, by dying." (*Shakespeare's Wordplay,* p. 72)

Likewise, Juliet ends with both conscious and unconscious wordplay. "Poison, I see, hath been his timeless end" (l. 162), she says, playing on the senses "untimely" and "endless, eternal." Her final words carry an erotic suggestion that echoes Romeo's:

> O happy dagger,
> This is thy sheath; [*Stabs herself.*] there rust, and let me die. (ll. 169–70)[44]

Here, "happy" equals fortunate, in being ready to hand, as well as successful, with a further quibble on "die" (i.e., reach sexual climax), as the action in sheathing the knife within her body suggests. "Death has long been Romeo's rival," Mahood says, "and enjoys Juliet at the last" (ibid., p. 58).

NOTES

1. For a detailed analysis of the metrics in this sonnet, see John Russell Brown, *Shakespeare's Dramatic Style* (New York: Barnes and Noble, 1972), pp. 40–44. Cp. Ralph Berry, *The Shakespearean Metaphor* (Totowa, N.J.: Rowman and Littlefield, 1978), p. 37: "The sonnet is the channel through which the play flows." He notes the sonnets and parts of sonnets that appear elsewhere in the play and help establish Verona as "a country of the mind, a locale whose inhabitants place themselves through their mode of discourse." On p. 39, Berry lists the various sonnet sequences influenced by Petrarch that preceded the composition of *Romeo and Juliet,* such as Sidney's *Astrophel and Stella* (1591), Samuel Daniel's *Delia* (1592), Barnabe Barnes's *Parthenophil and Parthenope* (1593), and so forth.

2. See Rosalie L. Colie, *Shakespeare's Living Art* (Princeton, N.J.: Princeton University Press, 1974), pp. 138–40, for analysis of Romeo's speeches in this scene. See also Jill Levenson, "The Definition of Love: Shakespeare's Phrasing in *Romeo and Juliet,*" *Shakespeare Studies* 15 (1982): 21–36. In Levenson's view, the material of amatory poetry pervades the tragedy as a whole; on the literary level, *Romeo and Juliet* is "one of Shakespeare's most analytical plays, an anatomy of love poetry" (p. 22). Cp. Ann Pasternak Slater, "Petrarchanism Come True in *Romeo and Juliet,*" in *Images of Shakespeare,* ed. Werner Habicht, D. J. Palmer, and Roger Pringle (Newark: University of Delaware Press, 1988), pp. 129–50. Slater argues that "Petrarchanism is central to the entire play—that in the love of Romeo and Juliet the empty paradoxes and hyperboles of Romeo's love for Rosaline become actual fact" (p. 129).

3. Cp. G. B. Evans, ed., *New Cambridge Shakespeare* (Cambridge: Cambridge University Press, 1984), p. 17. Similarly, Wolfgang Clemen notes Capulet's conventional language as a character trait, for example, at 3.5.126–38; see *The Development of Shakespeare's Imagery,* 2nd ed. (London: Methuen, 1977), pp. 63–64.

4. See Harry Levin, "Form and Formality in *Romeo and Juliet,*" in *"Romeo and Juliet": Critical Essays,* ed. John F. Andrews (New York: Garland, 1993), p. 44. He argues that when Juliet is at one with Romeo, her intonations are genuine; when she is at odds with him, they are unconvincing.

5. See G. R. Hibbard, *The Making of Shakespeare's Dramatic Poetry* (Toronto: University of Toronto Press, 1981), pp. 130–32, on Old Capulet's speeches. Cp. Robert O. Evans, *The Osier Cage* (Lexington: University of Kentucky Press, 1966), p. 44, who makes a similar point about Friar Lawrence's soliloquy that opens 2.3.

6. Colie, *Shakespeare's Living Art,* p. 140.

7. Richard David, *The Janus of the Poets* (Cambridge: Cambridge University Press, 1935), p. 23. Cp. Edward Snow, "Language and Sexual Difference in *Romeo and Juliet,*" in *Shakespeare's "Rough Magic,"* ed. Peter Erickson and Coppélia Kahn (Newark: University of Delaware Press, 1985), pp. 168–92. Snow shows that, their many links notwithstanding, the language Romeo and Juliet use is differentiated by their sex. For example, Romeo's "imaginative universe" is dominated by eyesight; his metaphors assemble reality "out there" and tend to make him sound more like an onlooker than a participant (p. 170). Juliet's imaginative universe, by contrast, is generated by all the senses and by a unity of feeling. Her images are of "whole, embodied selves, and extravagant gestures of giving and taking" (p. 173). Her desire functions as "an *erotic* reality-principle" that counteracts a "wistfulness" ingrained in Romeo (p. 176).

8. Berry, *Shakespearean Metaphor*, p. 39. Cp. Edgar Mertner, " 'Conceit Brags of His Substance, Not of Ornament': Some Notes on Style in *Romeo and Juliet*," in *Shakespeare: Text, Language, Criticism,* ed. B. Fabian and K. T. von Rosador (Hildesheim, Germany: Olms-Weidmann, 1987), pp. 186–87: "The sonnet with its clever arrangement of voices, the blending of wit and intellectual power with genuine feeling, of real love with playful flirting, of passion with well-bred manners, is one of the most brilliant feats of poetic conceit ever written."

9. As noted by Colie, *Shakespeare's Living Art*, p. 142.

10. Clemen, *Development*, pp. 64–68. Not all critics agree with this view. See, for example, Mertner, "Some Notes on Style," pp. 184–85. On the other hand, most recognize that even when Romeo and Juliet use conventional language, they have earned the right to do so; it is no longer artificial in the same sense as, say, Romeo's use of Petrarchan expression apropos of Rosaline. Cp. Colie, *Shakespeare's Living Art,* p. 143: "petrarchan [*sic*] language, *the* vehicle for amorous emotion, can be used merely as the cliché which Mercutio and Benvolio criticize; or, it can be earned by a lover's experience of the profound oppositions to which [the] rhetoric of oxymoron points."

11. According to Evans, *The Osier Cage,* Juliet is Romeo's master (p. 41) and instructs him in the extraordinary nature of their relationship (p. 52). Cp. Mertner's analysis of a brief but similar situation, 2.6.24–34 ("Some Notes on Style," p. 188).

12. For an analysis of the four "movements" in this scene, and of the way they are framed by the irreverence of Mercutio's "preface" (2.1) and the Friar's earthy soliloquy (2.3), see Douglas Cole's introduction to his edited collection *Twentieth Century Interpretations of "Romeo and Juliet"* (Englewood Cliffs, N.J.: Prentice-Hall, 1970), pp. 8–10.

13. Hibbard, *Making of Shakespeare's Dramatic Poetry,* p. 124. Brian Gibbons (New Arden edition [London: Methuen, 1980], p. 50) notes the "increasing distance" between the lovers' "earlier poetic artifice and their present experience."

14. Colie, *Shakespeare's Living Art,* p. 145. Cp. Shakespeare's use of the aubade in *Troilus and Cressida* 4.2.1–18, where the lovers are not married.

15. Berry, *Shakespearean Metaphor,* p. 38.

16. Cp. Gibbons, New Arden edition, p. 49, who notes that after the garden scene (2.2), rhyme becomes associated chiefly with formality, as in the Friar's first scene (2.3), the Prince's speech at the end of 3.1, and Paris's sestet at 5.3.12–17.

17. Hibbard, *Making of Shakespeare's Dramatic Poetry,* p. 125.

18. To cite just one example: in *The Merchant of Venice* 2.2, Bassanio speaks in blank verse and Launcelot Gobbo in prose. In *Romeo and Juliet,* too, Romeo and Benvolio in 1.2 speak in verse, while Capulet's servant speaks in prose.

19. David, *Janus of Poets,* p. 29, and Hibbard, *Making of Shakespeare's Dramatic Poetry,* pp. 125–27. Both of these scholars note that the Nurse's speeches in this scene were printed in the early quartos as prose, possibly because tradition was too strong for the compositors, who knew, or thought they knew, that the Nurse should speak in prose. For further analysis of her speech, see James Sutherland, "How the Characters Talk," in *Shakespeare's World,* ed. James Sutherland and Joel Hurstfield (London: Edward Arnold, 1964), pp. 127–28, and especially Stanley Wells, "Juliet's Nurse: The Uses of Inconsequentiality," in *Shakespeare's Styles,* ed. Philip Edwards, Inga-Stina Ewbank, and G. K. Hunter (Cambridge: Cambridge University Press, 1980), pp. 51–66. Wells notes that the Nurse's speech occurs within the play's "rich stylistic diversity" that helps establish style as a guide to character and encourages us to respond to verbal effects rather than plot development, which here is less important (pp. 58–59).

20. *Gammer Gurton's Needle* and Nicholas Udall's *Ralph Roister Doister* immediately come to mind.

21. I am indebted to E. Pearlman's unpublished paper, "Shakespeare at Work: Colloquial Conversation," which analyzes in detail the conversation of the cousins and its contrast with Romeo's lines. On Shakespeare's "continuously varied and responsive blank verse," see also Sutherland, "How the Characters Talk," p. 131. He discerns "a contrapuntal effect between the formal rhythm of the pentameter line and the rhythm of colloquial speech," for example, in the dialogue between Tybalt and Capulet at 1.5.64–91.

22. Milton Crane, *Shakespeare's Prose* (Chicago: University of Chicago Press, 1951), p. 137.

23. Ibid., p. 139. Cp. Berry, *Shakespearean Metaphor,* p. 41: "Mercutio himself has a profound contempt for rhyme; he can scarcely bring himself to perpetrate a single one. His mode is a supple, virile prose, or a liberated blank verse; but preferably prose."

24. Crane, *Shakespeare's Prose,* p. 141.

25. For example, Snug the joiner, Flute the bellows-mender, and Snout the tinker. Peter Quince's name derives from *quines,* or *quoins,* wooden wedges used by carpenters; Bottom the weaver's name comes from *bottom,* the core on which the weaver's skein of yarn was wound. See Harold Brooks, ed., *A Midsummer Night's Dream,* New Arden edition (London: Methuen, 1979), p. 3.

26. Brian Vickers, *The Artistry of Shakespeare's Prose* (London: Methuen, 1968), p. 74.

27. Caroline Spurgeon, *Shakespeare's Imagery and What It Tells Us* (Cambridge: Cambridge University Press, 1935), p. 310.

28. In *Shakespeare's Imagery,* app. 4, pp. 364–67, Spurgeon gives a full list of images by category (e.g., Nature, Personification, Animals) and subcategory, with a brief analysis. She counts 204 images in the play, as compared with 279 in *Hamlet.* See also Marion Bodwell Smith, *Dualities in Shakespeare* (Toronto: University of Toronto Press, 1966), pp. 79–109, for further detailed discussion of Shakespeare's images, for example, the death/marriage bed imagery, the sea imagery, and the imagery of blighted blossoms in the play.

29. Cp. Colie, *Shakespeare's Living Art,* p. 145, where she describes Shakespeare's ability to "unmetaphor" literary devices—that is, his talent for the "sinking of conventions back into what, he somehow persuades us, is 'reality.' " She cites as one example this scene, the *hortus conclusus,* the enclosed garden, which by metaphoric convention a virgin is and in which pure love naturally dwells. Juliet's balcony opens on an enclosed or walled garden, where the virgin is—and is *in*—it. The conventionality is forgotten as it is unmetaphored by the action that follows.

30. Clemen, *Development,* pp. 72–73.

31. See, for example, F. E. Halliday, *The Poetry of Shakespeare's Plays* (London: Duckworth, 1954), p. 92.

32. See, for example, Harold Goddard, *The Meaning of Shakespeare* (Chicago: University of Chicago Press, 1951), pp. 123–24, who justifies the speech, arguing that Shakespeare uses it to show what poetry is *not* (as compared with the poetry the lovers speak), even as it outshines most of the verse of the Capulets and Friar Lawrence.

33. Halliday, *Poetry,* p. 92. Indeed, as Joseph Porter suggests, Mercutio himself seems almost carried away by it, as if possessed by the god, or classical deliverer, of dreams (*Shakespeare's Mercutio* [Chapel Hill: University of North Carolina Press, 1988], pp. 104–5).

34. Maynard Mack, *Everybody's Shakespeare* (Lincoln: University of Nebraska Press, 1993), p. 77.

35. The transition between her two activities is the soldier's dreams (ll. 82–88), which frighten him so that he awakens.

36. Cited by M. M. Mahood, *Shakespeare's Wordplay* (London: Methuen, 1957), p. 9. Much of the following discussion is indebted to her chapter on *Romeo and Juliet,* pp. 56–72.

37. As Slater notes, dramatic irony pervades the play. Even relatively minor characters, like Friar Lawrence and Tybalt, have premonitions of a tragic outcome. "Whenever characters indulge in outrageous literary hyperbole," she says, "the plot takes them at their word" ("Petrarchanism Come True," p. 133).

38. This is the Q1 reading. The modern emendation most editors adopt, "open-arse," emended from Q2/F "open, or," destroys the innuendo.

39. Cp. similar wordplay in *1 Henry IV* 3.3.110–30. The kinship between Mistress Quickly and the Nurse has often been remarked.

40. See Jill Levenson, "Shakespeare's *Romeo and Juliet*: The Places of Invention," *Shakespeare Survey* 49 (1996): 51–52. Throughout her article (pp. 45–55), Levenson discusses Shakespeare's use of rhetorical devices and compares it to its use in his sources.

41. Cp. Vickers, *Artistry,* p. 72, who explains Mercutio's bawdry and the Nurse's as Shakespeare's "recurrent desire to separate the purely physical appetite from his nobler lovers and locate it somewhere else." But he feels that their humor bulks too large in the play and that its deflating tendency is often too violent (p. 73).

42. See, for example, Elbow's puns, as well as his malapropism (another indication of his stress), in *Measure for Measure* 2.1.41–67. Cp. Mahood, *Shakespeare's Wordplay,* p. 70, who says Juliet's wordplay in the passage that follows is "one of Shakespeare's first attempts to reveal a profound disturbance of mind by the use of quibbles."

43. As glossed by Gibbons, New Arden edition.

44. Snow, "Language and Sexual Difference," p. 190 n. 9, prefers the Q1 reading "rest" instead of the Q2/F "rust." He compares Romeo's reference to his "everlasting rest" (5.3.110) and provides other arguments in favor of "rest" as the better term in this context.

6

THEMES

Untypically, Shakespeare begins *Romeo and Juliet* with a Prologue, spoken by the Chorus, which announces several of the play's major themes: (1) the feud, or "ancient grudge," between two households; (2) the "star-crossed" lovers; (3) their "death-marked" love; and (4) the sacrifice their love makes. These are not the play's only themes; as rich in language as *Romeo and Juliet* is, so is it also rich in thematic development.[1] The themes intersect at different points in the action, with the various image patterns and with the interplay of characters. More typically, Shakespeare's plays suggest thematic concerns through the initial dialogue; hence, when Sampson and Gregory pun on *coals/colliers/choler/collar*, they indicate not only the blinding hatred that everyone—from the lowest to the highest level, the servants to the masters—must bear, but the penalties, too, that are potentially involved in this behavior.[2] As their dialogue continues, their preoccupation with male sexuality in its animal mode, another theme in the play, emerges. It is taken up later by Mercutio and contrasted with the loftier experience of love by Romeo and Juliet. Finally, Sampson's boast that he will cut off the heads of the maids, or their maidenheads (ll. 19–22), points forward to Juliet's marriage with Romeo and their mutual deflowering, as anticipated in Juliet's soliloquy in 3.2. There she refers to losing "a pair of stainless maidenhoods" (l. 13), realized that evening, but in a manner far different from the way the Capulet servant intends.

THE "ANCIENT GRUDGE" AND THE "STAR-CROSSED LOVERS"

Critical opinion divides over the nature of Romeo and Juliet's tragedy and the extent to which it is or is not a tragedy of fate or fortune. At a number of places in the text, both Romeo and Juliet themselves express presentiments of disaster, as if they were propelled by a force greater than themselves. Before entering the ball and seeing Juliet for the first time, Romeo remarks:

> my mind misgives
> Some consequence yet hanging in the stars
> Shall bitterly begin his fearful date
> With this night's revels, and expire the term
> Of a despisèd life closed in my breast,
> By some vile forfeit of untimely death. (1.4.106–11)

In the first balcony scene, Juliet, too, has some misgivings, but she attributes them to the rashness of their actions, not to the stars' dominion:

> I have no joy of this contract tonight,
> It is too rash, too unadvised, too sudden,
> Too like lightning, which doth cease to be
> Ere one can say 'It lightens'. (2.2.117–20)

Romeo persists, however, in believing that "black fate" has had a hand in subsequent events and will continue to have (3.1.110). He is "fortune's fool" (3.1.127), he laments, after killing Tybalt. Later, hearing of Juliet's supposed death, he says, "Is it e'en so? then I defy you, stars!" (5.1.24). On the other hand, at his first foreboding of disaster, he concludes: "But He that hath the steerage of my course / Direct my sail!" (1.4.112–13). Moreover, it is to Friar Lawrence, his "ghostly sire," that he repairs immediately after bidding good-night to Juliet in the garden; and like a good Christian gentleman, he wants to be "combined" with Juliet in "holy marriage" (2.3.60–61).

How may these apparently conflicting references be resolved? To what extent are Romeo and Juliet victims of some blind fate? To what extent does their tragedy result from their freely chosen actions? One solution to this critical dilemma is to take references to the stars and fortune figuratively, as metaphors. But in doing so, can one ignore another element—chance—that has a direct effect upon what happens to the lovers? Friar Lawrence's letter to Romeo miscarries because Friar John stops to ask another of their order to accompany him to Mantua and winds up in quarantine with him instead (5.2.4–12). Romeo arrives at the tomb and drinks the poison seconds before Friar Lawrence comes and Juliet awakens. These are not mere coincidences but seem to be the direct effect of a malevolent destiny, making the lovers appear star-crossed indeed.[3]

Franklin M. Dickey resolves the critical dilemma by regarding fortune not as a prime mover of human destiny, but the agent of a higher power. "If fortune is not the independent cause of the catastrophe, then we must look behind fortune for the actions which set it in motion," he says.[4] Throughout the swiftly moving play, we are aware of the hastiness with which the lovers act. Juliet's misgivings, cited above, are justified and reinforced in the very next scene by Friar Lawrence, who cautions Romeo, "Wisely and slow, they stumble that run fast" (2.3.94). Again, before Juliet enters in 2.6, he warns:

These violent delights have violent ends,
And in their triumph die like fire and powder,
Which as they kiss, consume. The sweetest honey
Is loathsome in his own deliciousness,
And in the taste confounds the appetite.
Therefore love moderately, long love doth so;
Too swift arrives as tardy as too slow. (ll. 9–15)

Friar Lawrence here seems to caution against an overhasty love that will destroy it-self—not as Romeo and Juliet are actually destroyed, but as love too soon con-summated may burn itself out. Nevertheless, "violent delights" often do have "violent ends" in ways other than he suspects.

But love is not the only prominent passion in the play. Hate is also powerfully represented, as Dickey takes pains to show (*Not Wisely,* pp. 95–101), particularly in the character of Tybalt. If the patriarchs of the two feuding houses appear as comic figures in the opening scene, they nonetheless support the brawl by their willingness to engage in the fray themselves. Hatred permeates much of the at-mosphere from beginning to end; it is in this context that the love between Romeo and Juliet emerges, and it is in the same context that their deaths occur. Tybalt seems to take special delight in being choleric, and only Capulet's forceful insis-tence restrains him from attacking Romeo during the ball scene. But he defers, does not forget, his anger at the perceived insult to the House of Capulet that Romeo's presence seems to signify, and so he sends Romeo a written challenge. His "violent delight" has its own "violent end" when, after killing Mercutio, he fights Romeo and is himself killed.

Tybalt's hatred arouses Romeo's, ironically, as only moments before they had become related through marriage. In vain Romeo pleads with Tybalt to stop trying to foment a quarrel between them; in the process he only succeeds in arousing Mercutio's ire. Anger breeds anger, and within minutes two men lie dead on the ground. Romeo himself risks death but instead receives banishment, which he ini-tially feels is a sentence worse than death. Nor does the hatred end there. Juliet's mother vents her spleen against Romeo, ironically foreshadowing the end of the play when she promises to find someone to poison Romeo (3.5.90) and when, shortly afterward, exasperated by Juliet's refusal to marry Paris, she cries, "I would the fool were married to her grave" (l. 140). If fate speaks through Juliet's mother, as Dickey maintains (*Not Wisely,* p. 100), it is fate conveyed through hate, the human passion, that precipitates the actions resulting in human catastrophe.

Passion, then, lies at the heart of this tragedy and is its prime mover. The dangers of passion were very much alive to Shakespeare's contemporaries, who repeatedly counseled that reason should control emotion. "Give me that man / That is not pas-sion's slave," Hamlet says to a stolid Horatio, "and I will wear him / In my heart's core, ay, in my heart of heart, / As I do thee" (3.2.71–74). Self-control is the burden of most of Friar Lawrence's counsel to Romeo, not only when he wails in despair at his banishment, but throughout his meetings with the young man. Excessive passion, however, is not Romeo's fault alone. Tybalt's irascibility and Mercutio's fiery temper also demonstrate the danger uncontrolled passion involves—to say nothing of the passions that are aroused among all the others in the first scene. On the other hand, how far can we blame the passion that Romeo and Juliet feel for each other, that not only moves them to ignore the prohibitions that their families' feud requires, to risk everything for each other, but that also brings them to surrender life itself if they cannot live together?[5]

If the love they share is not the culprit, then it is the hasty actions they take, especially Romeo's, that precipitate the tragedy. True, love motivates their actions, basically, but not wholly. An impatience, an impetuosity, characteristic of youth, also propels them. Heedless of the Friar's warnings and of Juliet's own initial fear that everything is proceeding too quickly, the lovers nevertheless move swiftly to determine their own destiny, thus allowing themselves to be carried away by their passion. This in part explains why Francis Fergusson links Shakespeare's play with canto 5 of Dante's *Inferno*, the Paolo-Francesca episode.[6] Both Dante and Shakespeare show how dangerous romantic love can be if obeyed literally before one fully understands it and its meanings. While it may be life-giving, as Friar Lawrence recognizes, it will be only for those who take time to hang on to it and find its deeper understandings. Though they know intuitively that their ghostly father is right, events move too fast for Romeo and Juliet, and all they actually experience is the love they feel for each other—and the deep despair that their frustrated love finally brings them, which leads directly to the catastrophe.

If Romeo was once willing to let a higher power direct his sail (1.4.113), at the end he is not; he takes everything into his own hands. In so doing, he cooperates with fate or chance as an agent of the higher power. Isolated in Mantua, he lacks the benefit of the Friar's counsel and therefore proceeds to that most heinous sin, suicide. Though commentators may moralize, as Arthur Brooke does in his poem, Shakespeare does not, either here or earlier when Romeo commits a series of disastrous errors.[7] In killing Paris before he takes his own life, he is guilty of another sin committed under the influence of his desperate passion.[8] And insofar as his suicide is the immediate cause of Juliet's, he is to that extent guilty of her death as well. Romeo claims that in taking his life he is shaking off the "yoke of inauspicious stars" (5.3.111). Is he? Or is he, like the desperate young man he is—and knows he is—attributing to fate problems that are at least in part, if not wholly, of his own making?[9]

THE "DEATH-MARKED" LOVE

Perhaps, as Norman Rabkin claims, Shakespeare's *Romeo and Juliet* tells us that "love, the most intense manifestation of the urge to life, is ineluctably linked with the self-destructive yearning for annihilation that we recognize as the death wish."[10] Like Shakespeare's poem *Venus and Adonis* earlier and *Antony and Cleopatra* later, *Romeo and Juliet* offers a perception that looks back toward the medieval romance tradition and forward to the works of Richard Wagner and Sigmund Freud. The intensity of the love that Romeo and Juliet share in itself predicts that disaster is practically inevitable, as through their presentiments they seem to realize. Death stalks them from the very outset. Before they even meet, a bloody riot occurs; "purple fountains" issuing from the veins of Montagues and Capulets alike cause the Prince to threaten both sides with pain of death if the civil peace is broken again (1.1.75–88).[11] At the ball, as soon as Romeo learns Juliet's name, he exclaims: "Is she a Capulet? / O dear account! my life is my foe's debt" (1.5.116–17). Juliet, too, sees the possibility of doom:

> My only love sprung from my only hate!
>
> .   .   .   .
>
> Prodigious birth of love it is to me,
> That I must love a loathèd enemy. (1.5.137–40)

The idea of death pervades their thoughts almost constantly. In the garden scene, Juliet reminds Romeo that where he is standing is "a place of death," considering who he is (2.2.64). Nothing daunted by the physical possibility of death, Romeo gallantly proclaims "there lies more peril in thine eye / Than twenty of their swords" (ll. 71–72). From the first, Romeo establishes his priorities: "My life were better ended by their hate, / Than death prorogued, wanting of thy love" (ll. 77–78). In proclaiming Romeo "the god of my idolatry" (l. 114), Juliet also commits herself fully to him, willing as his wife to lay all her fortunes at his foot and follow him as lord "throughout the world" (ll. 147–48), whatever the risks. Her trope at the end of the scene unconsciously foretells their fate:

> JULIET   'Tis almost morning, I would have thee gone:
> And yet no farther than a wanton's bird,
> That lets it hop a little from his hand,
> Like a poor prisoner in his twisted gyves,
> And with a silken thread plucks it back again,
> So loving-jealous of his liberty.
>
> ROMEO   I would I were thy bird.
>
> JULIET   Sweet, so would I,
> Yet I should kill thee with much cherishing. (2.2.176–82)

Not only in their thoughts and speech, but in others' also, the idea of death is pervasive. Friar Lawrence's soliloquy in the scene immediately following is filled with ominous images of "frowning night," darkness reeling "like a drunkard," "baleful weeds," and earth both as "nature's mother" and "her tomb" (2.3.1ff.). The apparent contradiction in the last example, carried forward throughout the rest of his speech, suggests what Rabkin calls Shakespeare's "complementary vision," his ability to see opposing aspects in complex human experience, often held together in unresolvable tensions.[12] As the play develops this theme, at the end

Romeo and Juliet seem to lose everything; from another point of view, they gain all that there is to be gained as their love reaches its apotheosis. The idea of complementarity, then, helps us to understand death not as annihilation, but as fulfillment too—an aspect of the theme to which we must return.

Meanwhile, death continues to stalk the lovers, subtly and indirectly throughout the rest of act 2 until it takes center stage in act 3 and reverses the direction of the action. It appears in Mercutio's mocking description of Romeo's death—for love—when Benvolio ominously mentions Tybalt's challenge:

> Alas, poor Romeo, he is already dead, stabbed with a white wench's black
> eye, run through the ear with a love-song, the very pin of his heart cleft with
> the blind bow-boy's butt-shaft. (2.4.13–15)

Mercutio, of course, is mistaken, at least in thinking that Romeo is still smitten by Rosaline, and the rest of the scene, especially when Romeo enters and later the Nurse and Peter, is full of high spirits. The next scene, too, is comic, but even there death's presence is felt. Impatient for her Nurse's return, Juliet complains that "old folks, many feign as they were dead, / Unwieldy, slow, heavy, and pale as lead" (2.5.16–17); and indeed, when she enters, the Nurse enacts precisely what Juliet has described, deliberately withholding for a while the good news she brings.

The ambivalence that Friar Lawrence expressed earlier emerges again in 2.6, as he and Romeo await Juliet's arrival to be married. Concerned (as he should be) over what he is about to undertake, he says: "So smile the heavens upon this holy act, / That after-hours with sorrow chide us not" (ll. 1–2). But Romeo spurns that concern with characteristic bravado:

> Amen, amen! but come what sorrow can,
> It cannot countervail the exchange of joy
> That one short minute gives me in her sight.
> Do thou but close our hands with holy words,
> Then love-devouring Death do what he dare,
> It is enough I may but call her mine. (ll. 3–8)

Romeo's words epitomize the tragedy that unfolds. The young man's eagerness to consummate his love frightens the Friar, who warns: "These violent delights have violent ends" (ll. 9–10). Juliet then enters, and he comments, with perhaps more ambiguity than he realizes: "O, so light a foot / Will ne'er wear out the everlasting flint." Indeed it will not, not that it ever could, of course. But a subsidiary meaning implies that the lovers will never last the course, beset by difficulties as they are.[13]

Death as a bridegroom becomes a leitmotiv in much of the rest of the play after Romeo kills Tybalt. Juliet's words after her initial meeting with Romeo become prophetic, though not for the reason she fears: "If he be marrièd, / My grave is like to be my wedding bed" (1.5.133–34). When she learns of Romeo's banishment, she naturally becomes distraught: "to speak that word, / Is father, mother, Tybalt, Romeo, Juliet, / All slain, all dead" (3.2.122–24). Resigned to her unhappy fate, she concludes, if somewhat prematurely, "I'll to my wedding-bed, / And death, not Romeo, take my maidenhead!" (ll. 136–37).

For Romeo, too, banishment means death: "For exile hath more terror in his look, / Much more than death," he wails in the Friar Lawrence's cell; "banishèd / Is death mistermed" (3.3.13–14, 20–21). It is all that the Friar and the Nurse can do to stop him from suicide then and there. The opportunity to see Juliet once more and to consummate their marriage heartens him. But when they part after their night of love, Juliet has dire forebodings as she watches Romeo descend from her balcony:

> O God, I have an ill-divining soul!
> Methinks I see thee now, thou art so low.
> As one dead in the bottom of a tomb. (3.5.54–56)

Juliet's mother also speaks more prophetically than she realizes when, angered at Juliet's refusal to consider marriage to Paris, she says: "I would the fool were married to her grave" (3.5.140). When her parents discover her apparently lifeless body after she takes the potion, Old Capulet mourns her with these words to Paris, who has come to carry his bride to church:

> O son, the night before thy wedding day
> Hath Death lain with thy wife. There she lies,
> Flower as she was, deflowerèd by him.
> Death is my son-in-law, Death is my heir,
> My daughter he hath wedded. I will die,
> And leave him all; life, living, all is Death's. (4.5.35–40)

The metaphor of death as a lover or bridegroom, here explicitly stated, is reprised afterward in the tomb as Romeo contemplates his beloved:

> Ah, dear Juliet,
> Why art thou yet so fair? Shall I believe
> That unsubstantial Death is amorous,
> And that the lean abhorrèd monster keeps
> Thee here in dark to be his paramour?
> For fear of that, I still will stay with thee,
> And never from this palace of dim night
> Depart again. (5.3.101–8)

Moments later, by sheathing his dagger in her body, Juliet carries the metaphor to a practically literal conclusion (5.3.170).

THE LOVERS' SACRIFICE

The love between Romeo and Juliet brings about the reconciliation of the feuding families, the Capulets and the Montagues, as the Friar wished (2.3.91–92), though not in the way he wished it. After hearing the Friar's account of events leading up to and including the lovers' deaths, Prince Escalus confirms the narrative with Romeo's letter (5.3.286). He then pronounces the paradoxical conclusion to the families' feud:

> Where be these enemies? Capulet, Montague?
> See what a scourge is laid upon your hate,
> That heaven finds means to kill your joys with love! (ll. 291–93)

Properly chastened, Capulet reaches out to Montague:

> O brother Montague, give me thy hand.
> This is my daughter's jointure, for no more
> Can I demand. (ll. 296–98)

Juliet's "jointure," or marriage settlement the bridegroom's father offers, is the handclasp of friendship he asks of his ancient enemy.

What a terrible price both families have paid—and Prince Escalus, for he has lost "a brace of kinsmen" (Mercutio and Paris), because of the enmity between the houses. Montague promises to raise a statue of Juliet in "pure gold,"

> That whiles Verona by that name is known,
> There shall be no figure at such rate be set
> As that of true and faithful Juliet. (ll. 299–302)

To which Capulet responds:

> As rich shall Romeo's as his lady's be,
> Poor sacrifices of our enmity! (ll. 304–5)

Both old men recognize, then, the sacrificial nature of their children's death. "All are punished," as the Prince says. The blood feud has taken the flower of Verona's youth to end it.

Not emphasized in these final moments, or even mentioned (though noted earlier by Capulet, 4.5.63–64), is that, with the deaths of Romeo and Juliet, the families' lineage ends. Romeo was the Montagues' only child; Juliet the Capulets' only surviving heir (1.2.14).[14] The feud has indeed killed all their joys, ironically, through love—the love of the young people that finally brings about love, or at least friendship, among the older generation. The deaths of Romeo and Juliet, as Brian Gibbons remarks, is a "sacrificial ritual . . . to purge Verona of its disease."[15] The disease, as the audience sees from the very beginning, is costly in both blood and lives. Prince Escalus's attempts to cure it prove vain, despite his strong warnings and threats. Much more seems to be required, and it is finally paid.[16]

That is one way of interpreting the death of the lovers. Another way of looking at what finally happens to them is to see Romeo and Juliet as winners, not losers or sacrificers to a world that they have in so many respects rejected in favor of what each means to the other. Through their deaths they have preserved the integrity of their love in a world that would destroy it. As in *1 Henry IV,* Shakespeare plays off the daytime world of affairs, work, and history against the nighttime world of romance, pleasure, and love. In the daytime world, time rules: in that world, typically a father becomes preoccupied with setting the date for his daughter's wedding, as old Capulet does regarding Juliet's marriage to Paris (3.4.18–30). In the nighttime world, time is forgotten—until day breaks, as it does in 3.5, and Romeo and Juliet must part after their night of love. Both worlds have their validity and complement each other even as they appear incompatible with each other.

Thus, as Rabkin says, it may be that "only annihilation can do full justice to such longings as Romeo and Juliet share."[17] The intensity of their love suggests that they could have no future in a world of "propagation and domestic contentment."[18] If their love reflects the classic literary statement of the *Liebestod* (love-death) myth, it may be, as M. M. Mahood suggests, because their *amour-passion* seeks satisfaction of forbidden desires—forbidden because (according to Freud) they are inimical to the race or because (according to Denis de Rougement) they are contrary to the faith.[19] On the other hand, their love is married love, not the adulterous love of the traditional myth. Romeo and Juliet want to live together, not die together—but on their own terms, not the terms that the world of their parents, Friar Lawrence, and others would impose upon them. They yearn to transform the world in a way that will correspond to their inner state. Failing that, anything less would be a betrayal of their love.[20]

Here it is important to recognize that Romeo and Juliet choose death; death does not simply happen to them. In death they find the only fulfillment of their love left to them. The toast Romeo utters as he drinks the poison is not bravado; the kiss he gives Juliet is "righteous"—sealing his "dateless bargain to engrossing Death!" (5.3.114–15). The dagger that Juliet kills herself with is a "happy dagger" (5.3.169). They do not die reluctantly; they die joyfully. Over Juliet's body, committing himself to his fate, Romeo says:

> O here
> Will I set up my everlasting rest,
> And shake the yoke of inauspicious stars
> From this world-wearied flesh. (5.3.109–12)

From one point of view, then, Romeo and Juliet lose everything; from another, they gain all that there is to be gained.[21] They are not merely sacrifices. The last words of the play, spoken by Prince Escalus, convey only part of the truth, the truth that his world, the daytime world, understands:

> For never was a story of more woe
> Than this of Juliet and Romeo.

THE BODY AND SEXUALITY

As *Romeo and Juliet* is one of Shakespeare's bawdiest plays, naturally it is also one filled with references to the physical world, particularly the body and its functions. The dialogue between Sampson and Gregory and what follows it—the vicious brawl between the Houses of Capulet and Montague—testify to humanity's vigorous physical life and the relation between violence and lust. The coarse talk of the servants generates, as Gibbons remarks, "an awareness of the body as an instrument of physical brutality and sexual aggression."[22] At the very beginning of the play, we are thus introduced to the lowest level of human behavior: its most animalistic tendencies. From this level, Shakespeare moves to the higher region of romantic love, but he never totally ignores basic urges and preoccupations. If the love between Romeo and Juliet rises to something loftier than animal lust, it nonetheless incorporates within that love a recognition, and indeed a celebration, of physical beauty and sexual consummation. The presence of Friar Lawrence may introduce the idea of male celibacy, with its reservations about the legitimacy of sexuality,[23] but if so, the idea is so deeply submerged that it never becomes thematic.

It emerges, rather, in what some have called a "religion of love"—profane love, of course—manifesting itself in the very first meeting between Romeo and Juliet. The young couple extend the conceit of religious palmers kissing, hand to hand, or palm to palm, at first, but then they move rapidly to lips touching:

ROMEO	If I profane with my unworthiest hand
	This holy shrine, the gentle sin is this,
	My lips, two blushing pilgrims, ready stand
	To smooth that rough touch with a tender kiss.
JULIET	Good pilgrim, you do wrong your hand too much,
	Which mannerly devotion shows in this,
	For saints have hands that pilgrims' hands do touch,
	And palm to palm is holy palmers' kiss.
ROMEO	Have not saints lips, and holy palmers too?
JULIET	Ay, pilgrim, lips that they must use in prayer.
ROMEO	O then, dear saint, let lips do what hands do:
	They pray, grant thou, lest faith turn to despair.
JULIET	Saints do not move, though grant for prayers' sake.
ROMEO	Then move not while my prayer's effect I take. (1.5.92–105)

This blending of the holy and the profane not only displays Romeo and Juliet's wit, but joins them from the outset in a love that is both physical and spiritual. Powerfully attracted to each other by beauty and sentiment, they are also moved by sexual impulses, expressed in the desire to touch lips as well as hands. Juliet is fully responsive here and later, though it is only as a bride that she will yield—quite gladly—to the ultimate consummation of their love.

Mercutio's and the Nurse's bawdy jests are the obverse side of Romeo and Juliet's interest in the body and sexuality, but in other ways, too, they show how preoccupied they are with bodily functions. When we first meet her, the Nurse delights in talking about how she gave the infant Juliet suck and weaned her from her dug (1.3.24–35). She is extremely conscious of her aches and pains, whose severity she probably exaggerates when she returns to Juliet and delays relating what Juliet earnestly wants to know (2.5.25–30, 47–51, 62). The comparison she makes between Romeo and Paris, moreover, concentrates almost entirely on their physical appearance (2.5.38–43). Mercutio pretends to care nothing for physical attraction, least of all his own, comparing his face to the grotesque visor he puts on for the ball (1.4.29–32). But like the Nurse, and as those lines indicate, he is almost obsessed with the body, especially as an instrument of sexual aggression: "If love be rough with you," he tells Romeo, "be rough with love: / Prick love for pricking, and you beat love down" (1.4.27–28). His Queen Mab speech is from the start mainly physical description, extremely detailed and precise, turning later to the effects of this fairy midwife's touch. The effects themselves involve physicalities, such as the blisters that plague ladies' lips (1.4.74–75) and the soldier's dream "of cutting foreign throats, / Of breaches, ambuscadoes, Spanish blades, / Of healths five fathom deep" (ll. 83–85). But his catalog ends, as for Mercutio it invariably does, with sexuality:

> This is the hag, when maids lie on their backs,
> That presses them and learns them first to bear,
> Making them women of good carriage. (ll. 92–94)..

The action of the play is highly physical as well, beginning with the swordplay in the opening scene. It continues to the Capulets' ball, where the masquers march around the stage (1.4.114 stage direction), servingmen are busy with their trenchers, musicians play, and party-goers dance. During this scene, Romeo and Juliet make their first physical contact, permitted by Capulet's restraint of Tybalt, who would engage Romeo in a duel then and there (1.5.53–91). Romeo leaps the garden wall in act 2 to catch a glimpse of Juliet, soon afterward climbing her balcony to engage her in amorous talk, while both are constantly aware of the physical danger should Romeo be discovered. When Romeo rejoins his friends the next day, Mercutio immediately describes him in physical terms: Romeo appears "[w]ithout his roe, like a dried herring. O flesh, flesh, how art thou fishified," he says (2.4.33–34). Before that, in conversation with Benvolio, Mercutio satirizes Tybalt's fencing techniques—a physical action that finds its climax, and the play's, in the next act.

The pivotal action of the entire play is that of the sword fights that occur first between Mercutio and Tybalt and then between Tybalt and Romeo. Tybalt has not forgotten his promise to wreak vengeance for the slight he feels Romeo has given the Capulets by crashing their party the night before. For his blood lust, he pays with his life. The duels themselves may be more or less vigorous, depending upon

the direction and, very likely, the fencing proficiency of the actors, but their phys-
icality should not be underestimated or underplayed. The cause of the duels links
the ancient theme of love and war, also significant in this play, to its other themes.
It also brings out the *odi-et-amo* (love-hate) motif, suggested earlier in Romeo's
Petrarchanism apropos of his infatuation with Rosaline,[24] but here developed more
seriously. Tybalt introduces the motif with his curious greeting: "Romeo, the love
I bear thee can afford / No better term than this: thou art a villain" (3.1.53–54).
Romeo counters with protests that he loves his enemy, Tybalt, more than he knows
or yet can know (ll. 55–58, 61–65). The scene ends, like the play, with Romeo
killing the thing he loves.

Physical display also characterizes much of the rest of the action. Romeo carries
on desperately in Friar Lawrence's cell (3.3), after which he once again, following
their night of love, climbs down from Juliet's balcony. Unlike modern films and
plays, Shakespeare felt no need to show the actual lovemaking; its aftermath was
more than sufficient and more to the point of the tragedy. It was enough that the
audience knew it had occurred. Instead, Shakespeare offers Juliet's epithalamium,
the kinetic energy of which fairly explodes from the verse. Earlier, Juliet had opposed her sensuous apprehension of her lover to the abstraction of his name. Compared to his physical attributes, his name meant nothing:

> 'Tis but thy name that is my enemy;
> Thou art thyself, though not a Montague.
> What's a Montague? It is not hand nor foot,
> Nor arm nor face, nor any other part
> Belonging to a man. (2.2.38–42)

Names are dispensable, or so she says, and Romeo agrees: "I take thee at thy word:
/ Call me but love, and I'll be new baptised" (ll. 49–50). Romeo's essence is not in
his name, but in his self, defined more by his personal attributes than by what he
is called. In her epithalamium, Juliet eagerly invites this Romeo, her husband, and
longs for the fulfillment of their love in these terms:

> O, I have bought the mansion of a love,
> But not possessed it, and though I am sold,
> Not yet enjoyed. (3.2.26–28)

And so to the end of the play: the second balcony scene and Romeo's descent;
Juliet's kneeling appeal to her father not to force her to marry Paris; her flight to
Friar Lawrence's cell and the potion she drinks despite her very real fears, con-
cretely imaged forth, of what awaits her in the tomb; and finally, the tomb itself.
There Romeo encounters Paris and, forced to draw, kills him before killing him-
self—but not before his apostrophe to Juliet's beauty:

> O my love, my wife,
> Death, that hath sucked the honey of thy breath,

Hath had no power yet upon thy beauty:
Thou art not conquered, beauty's ensign yet
Is crimson in thy lips and in thy cheeks,
And Death's pale flag is not advancèd there. (5.3.91–96)

When she awakens, Juliet, too, focuses on her lover's lips,[25] salutes his "timeless end," and cries:

O churl, drunk all, and left no friendly drop
To help me after? I will kiss thy lips,
Haply some poison yet doth hang on them,
To make me die with a restorative. (ll. 163–66)

Here, as in her last lines, Juliet deliberately chooses sexual and other ambiguities to make her valediction. The poison she hopes still remains on his lips will be a "restorative" to unite her with Romeo and thus let her "die" with him. Failing that, she takes his dagger and "sheathes" it in her body. The play's final symbolic gesture occurs, appropriately, as Capulet and Montague join hands and end their "ancient grudge."

NOTES

1. See, for example, Ann Pasternak Slater's discussion of the theme "All things change them to the contrary," in "Petrarchanism Come True in *Romeo and Juliet,*" in *Images of Shakespeare,* ed. Werner Habicht, D. J. Palmer, and Roger Pringle (Newark: University of Delaware Press, 1988), pp. 132–40. See also Gordon Ross Smith, "The Balance of Themes in *Romeo and Juliet,*" in *Essays on Shakespeare,* ed. Gordon Ross Smith (University Park: Pennsylvania State University Press, 1965), pp. 15–66. Smith discusses several levels of thematic development, such as the relationship of concupiscence, ireful passion, and reason, in the philosophical terms Shakespeare's contemporaries understood and in the modern equivalents of these terms.

2. The pun on *collar* alludes to the hangman's noose. Note that Tybalt, perhaps the most choleric among the characters, refers to his own "wilful choler" after Capulet restrains him from attacking Romeo at the ball (1.5.88).

3. Cp. Ruth Nevo, *Tragic Form in Shakespeare* (Princeton, N.J.: Princeton University Press, 1972), p. 32, who also notes how ill will and ill luck coalesce in Shakespeare's later tragedies, though not in *Romeo and Juliet.*

4. Franklin M. Dickey, *Not Wisely but Too Well* (San Marino: Huntington Library, 1957), p. 95. Cp. John F. Andrews, "Falling in Love: The Tragedy of *Romeo and Juliet,*" in *Classical, Renaissance, and Postmodernist Acts of the Imagination,* ed. Arthur Kinney (Newark: University of Delaware Press, 1996), p. 180: For Boethius and subsequent Christian philosophers, Fate was a term for a higher authority that presided over Fortune, or mutability (Chance). Fate was a pagan disguise for Providence, ultimately benign, though shrouded in obscurity.

5. Cp. Andrews, "Falling in Love," pp. 181–85, who cites Augustine's view that all movement of the soul is prompted by the will, and what moves the will is love. Augustine distinguishes between sacred love (*caritas*) and profane love (*cupiditas*). Romeo and Juliet's

love is a species of the latter, which they wrongly elevate to a form of "pseudo-worship." This is their tragic flaw.

6. See Francis Fergusson, *Trope and Allegory* (Athens: University of Georgia Press, 1977), pp. 7–22.

7. See Dickey, *Not Wisely,* pp. 114–16. Romeo's mistakes include becoming infatuated, choosing revenge when Tybalt kills Mercutio, falling into frantic despair at his banishment, and succumbing to complete despair when he learns of Juliet's entombment. He is a tragic hero like Othello, according to Dickey, insofar as he is responsible for his own chain of passionate actions. As against traditional interpretations of Shakespeare's tragedy, cp. Kiernan Ryan, "*Romeo and Juliet*: The Language of Tragedy," in *The Taming of the Text,* ed. Willie Van Peer (London: Routledge, 1988), pp. 107–21. Ryan argues: "By explaining *Romeo and Juliet* as a timeless and universal tragedy of the 'human condition', as the arbitrary result of mere chance, or as a consequence of the purely personal moral defects of the protagonists, criticism has conspired to evade or obscure the subversive utopian significance of their love and the play's indictment of the specific social forces which deny that love the right to exist and flourish" (pp. 108–9).

8. Dickey, *Not Wisely,* p. 115. This incident is not found in Brooke's poem.

9. See ibid., pp. 89–94, where fate and fortune are discussed in Shakespeare's work generally and in the overall context of Elizabethan attitudes toward astrology. Dickey argues that there is "no blind fate in Shakespearean tragedy or in the Elizabethan universe"; instead, the "unchanging ground of Shakespeare is the belief in a just Providence" (*Not Wisely,* p. 91).

10. Norman Rabkin, *Shakespeare and the Common Understanding* (New York: Free Press, 1967), p. 151. Cp. M. M. Mahood's discussion of the *Liebestod* (love-death) myth and its appearance in the play, in *Shakespeare's Wordplay* (London: Methuen, 1957), pp. 56–58, and Smith, "Balance of Themes," pp. 54–55, 60–61.

11. The scene has been variously played. In Franco Zeffirelli's film, the violence is fierce, and men die of sword wounds. But in keeping with the comic spirit of the play's opening, the brawl may be somewhat less horrendous, though vigorous enough to justify the Prince's remarks.

12. Rabkin, *Common Understanding,* p. 184. For Rabkin's definition of "complementarity" as a mode of awareness, see p. 27.

13. Mahood, *Shakespeare's Wordplay,* p. 62. As Mahood notes, still another sense ("ne'er" = "near") suggests that Juliet's luminous beauty and love will almost outlast the hardest physical substance.

14. Benvolio is related to the Montagues, but he disappears after act 3; and in Q1 we learn that he, like Lady Montague, has died.

15. Brian Gibbons, New Arden edition (London: Methuen, 1980), p. 72. Cp. Irving Ribner, *Patterns in Shakespearean Tragedy* (New York: Barnes and Noble, 1960), p. 27: "The elders must pay for their sins with the lives of their children." Ribner argues that Shakespeare imposed a Christian framework upon his story, though he recognizes the difficulty that the suicide of the lovers presents.

16. For the rhythms of ritual sacrifice in Shakespearean tragedy, see John Holloway's chapter "Shakespearean Tragedy and the Idea of Human Sacrifice," in *The Story of the Night* (London: Routledge and Kegan Paul, 1961), pp. 135–54. Although Holloway's analysis focuses mainly on the later tragedies, to which it is most directly relevant, his notion of the relationship between the individual and the community is generally applicable. He argues, for example, that to pursue an analogy between the experience offered by Shake-

speare's tragedies, on the one hand, and the rites of sacrifice, on the other, is to conclude that "a strengthening and deepening of the spectator's sense of community with his fellows may indeed be a major part of that experience" (p. 146). Cp. Marion Bodwell Smith, *Dualities in Shakespeare* (Toronto: University of Toronto Press, 1966), p. 97, who sees the play as "an adaptation of the archetypal myth in which youth and maiden are sacrificed for the peace and fertility of the state," an interpretation supported by the ubiquitous fertility imagery, the prevalence of sexual ambiguities, the religious imagery of the lovers, and other aspects of the play.

17. Rabkin, *Common Understanding,* p. 183.

18. Smith, Dualities, p. 97. Cp. Mahood, *Shakespeare's Wordplay,* p. 65: "The final victory of time and society over the lovers is counterpoised by the knowledge that it is, in a sense, *their* victory: a victory not only over time and society which would have made them old and worldly in the end (whereas their deaths heal the social wound), but over the most insidious enemy of love, the inner hostility that 'builds a Hell in Heaven's despite' and which threatens in the broad jests of Mercutio."

19. Mahood, *Shakespeare's Wordplay,* p. 58.

20. Rabkin, *Common Understanding,* p. 183. Cp. Marjorie Garber, *Dream in Shakespeare* (New Haven, Conn.: Yale University Press, 1974), pp. 44–47, on the interpretation of Romeo's dream in 5.1.1–11. Garber says that the prediction, that Juliet found him dead and then he "revived and was an emperor," ceases to be literal and becomes metaphorical. "Romeo's final dream brings him close to a poetic understanding of his own situation and makes him into an interpreter of the play as well as its protagonist" (p. 47).

21. Rabkin, *Common Understanding,* p. 184. Cp. Mahood, *Shakespeare's Wordplay,* p. 72, who also notes how poetry gives effect and value to incompatible meanings. In *Romeo and Juliet,* the use of paradox, the recurrent image, and other means contribute to this end; hence, the final emotion we feel is neither the satisfaction of a simple expression of the *Liebestod* theme nor the dismay of seeing two lives destroyed by vicious fate, but "a tragic equilibrium which includes and transcends both these feelings."

22. Gibbons, New Arden edition, p. 64.

23. Edward Snow, "Language and Sexual Difference in *Romeo and Juliet,*" in *Shakespeare's "Rough Magic,"* ed. Peter Erickson and Coppélia Kahn (Newark: University of Delaware Press, 1985), p. 187.

24. Mahood, *Shakespeare's Wordplay*, pp. 60–61.

25. A cursory glance through the concordance shows that whereas mention of various bodily parts associated with love poetry (e.g., cheeks, arms, face, hands, eyes) appear frequently in Shakespeare's poems and plays, including this one, lips seem more numerous in *Romeo and Juliet* than in any other play.

7

CRITICAL APPROACHES

The foregoing chapters have dwelt mainly upon traditional approaches to under-standing *Romeo and Juliet*. They have dealt with the historical materials Shake-speare used (source study), textual analysis, close reading, theme and structure analysis, and character and language study. Yet other, more specialized modern ap-proaches are also available. This chapter will give brief descriptions, together with some examples, of approaches based in psychoanalytical criticism, feminist and gender criticism, and myth and archetypal criticism.

PSYCHOANALYTICAL CRITICISM

Freudian psychology made its first and most potent impact on Shakespeare studies in Ernest Jones's *Hamlet and Oedipus* (1947). Since that time, many other plays by Shakespeare have come under scrutiny by psychoanalytically oriented critics, and *Romeo and Juliet* is no exception. Although Freudianism has come under attack, its influence is still felt, however modified it has been or its direction changed by Carl Jung, Alfred Adler, Jacques Lacan, and others. An early cham-pion of Freudian criticism specifically directed to Shakespeare studies was Nor-man Holland, whose book *Psychoanalysis and Shakespeare* (1966) is a clear, readable account of psychoanalytical theory and practice. "Psychoanalysis is that science," he says, "which tries to speak objectively about subjective states, specif-ically, subjective states resisted but arrived at in the psychoanalytic interview." He continues by quoting Freud: " 'The only subject matter of psychoanalysis is the mental processes of human beings and it is only in human beings that it can be studied.' "[1] Since characters in a drama are not, in fact, human beings with their own mental processes, but rather the products of another's, and since their as-sumed mental states cannot be studied in the psychoanalytic interview, psychoan-alytical interpretations of literature would seem to be impossible—an objection sometimes directed against literary critics who follow this approach.[2]

But if art is "a conventionally accepted reality in which, thanks to artistic illusion, symbols and substitutes are able to provoke real emotions," as Freud claims,[3] then a work of art is susceptible to psychoanalytical interpretation. Of course, Freud and, after him, Jones were really interested in exploring the mind of the author through the work of art, rather than the work of art itself.[4] The practical difficulties—the author, if dead, is unable to participate in a psychoanalytical interview—need not concern us here. Suffice it to say that some critics accept the "artistic illusion" as sufficiently "real" to justify the methods of psychoanalytical interpretation. They may not be and usually are not so much interested in the mind of the author as in gaining insights into the work the author has produced. "To use Freud's remarks on Shakespeare for literary purposes," Holland says, "we must turn them inside out, making his inductions deductive applications of general psychological principles to particular aspects of Shakespeare's plays and poems. When we do, we find his remarks are not without purely literary interest" (*Psychoanalysis,* p. 55).

According to the psychoanalytic view of art, Holland maintains (ibid., p. 78), the unconscious of the artist speaks to the unconscious of his or her audience. What does pscyhoanalytical criticism contribute to our understanding of *Romeo and Juliet*? Up to the mid-1960s, when *Psychoanalysis and Shakespeare* was published, the answer was, somewhat surprisingly, very little. In *Man against Himself* (1938), Karl A. Meninger argued that *Romeo and Juliet* was "a dramatic exposition of impulsiveness combining with hate to become self-destruction. . . . Romeo's impulsiveness causes Mercutio's death . . . [and] causes his own banishment when he impulsively kills Tybalt."[5] Similarly, his impulsiveness results in his and Juliet's suicides. Such impulsiveness, Meninger said, derives from "ill-controlled, partially disguised aggression." In 1954, L. A. Strong held a comparable view: Romeo suffered from a neurotic inability to tolerate separation in time and space, and from his neurosis stem the mistimings that eventuate in catastrophe.

In the 1940s, Theodore Reik's views of romantic love led him to analyze Romeo as someone who, when he met Juliet, was in a dangerous state of despair and depression as a result of Rosaline's rejection. In Juliet he found an ideal of himself, a person he wished to be like, or really be. This wish gives rise to feelings of envy, hostility, and possessiveness, and love is the reaction against that envy and hostility. The feud between the Montagues and the Capulets stands for the hate elements in love, which in turn emerge in Juliet's brief ambivalence after Romeo kills her cousin Tybalt. Note also Romeo's devaluation of himself, his willingness to doff his name, which, once he meets Juliet, becomes hateful to him (2.2.55). Projecting onto Juliet "ideals and aspirations, and not real values" harks back to a childish love for an all-powerful, all-loving parent; hence, such a lover constitutes an "incest object," a forbidden love. In Reik's view, Romeo's love is a childish shifting back and forth between a regression to narcissism and a childish identification with the loved one. Several years later in an article in *American Imago* (1957), Joseph L. Vredenburg restated Reik's insights.

Holland also summarizes Robert Fliess's analyses of the Nurse and Mercutio and extrapolates from them an interpretation of the play as one of "fragmented loves." Noting how Fliess speaks of Mercutio and the Nurse as if they were real people, Holland probes that issue with relevance to his own analysis of Romeo's dream in 5.1.6–9. He says:

> The dream is wholly and totally realistic in the sense that a psychological analysis shows it has all the properties a real dream has. It is sleep preserving; it is built out of "day residue"; it is a wish-fulfilling fantasy both in terms of Romeo's adult world and his hypothetical childhood at stages oral, phallic, and oedipal. But what sense does it make to speak of a "realistic" dream in so highly stylized and formal a work as *Romeo and Juliet*? (*Psychoanalysis*, pp. 265–66)

Holland's answer to his question is to see whether the psychological description of the event (or character) can be phrased in terms that apply to the total work, and for him "reversal" links the dream (analyzed as if it were a real dream) to the play around it. Romeo's dream prophesies (by reversal) his own death; it is also wish fulfillment that reverses his present loveless situation. He becomes an "emperor," further reversing his present outcast state. And so on. As for phallic symbolism (a staple of psychoanalytical criticism), his dream gives him "an inexhaustible potency, in which intercourse simply produces new erections." Finally, "at the deepest oral level," his dream turns Romeo's death into a rebirth: "he becomes the emperor-child-father whose mother thrusts life into his lips."

To the theater audience, this dream must seem a reversal, coming as it does *just before Romeo learns of his love's death*. But the psychological effect of the tragedy as a whole is also one of reversal, "the most exquisite expression of the child's wish for love"—Romeo and Juliet reversing their elders' old hatred. Holland concludes that Romeo's dream, even analyzed with the techniques of modern psychoanalytical criticism as though it were real, still fits into Shakespeare's highly stylized tragedy: "this is the paradox of literary realism" (ibid., p. 267). He further suggests that the theme of reversal, of swinging back and forth between diametric opposites, may have something to do with Shakespeare's attempts in other early plays, such as *Richard III*, to master erotic problems by political action and vice versa. The families' feud in *Romeo and Juliet* may be understood, then, as a political (or quasi-political) problem for Verona and the Prince to be mastered by erotic action.

Coppélia Kahn's now-classic essay "Coming of Age in Verona"[6] uses a psychoanalytical approach for several of her observations on *Romeo and Juliet* while showing how the young lovers mature in their feud-riven city. In her view, the feud is the primary tragic force in the play, not the feud as an agent of fate, but as "an extreme and peculiar expression of patriarchal society, which Shakespeare shows to be tragically self-destructive" (p. 337). Despite the lovers' attempt to create new identities for themselves, the feud effectively blocks Romeo and Juliet's best efforts. The feud socializes the young people of Verona in two ways: it reinforces their identities as sons and daughters of opposing households, thus polarizing all their social relations, particularly marital choices; and it provides a "psycho-sexual moratorium" for the sons, who must prove themselves by "phallic vio-lence" on behalf of their fathers, instead of a more natural courtship and sexual ex-perimentation leading toward marriage and separation from the paternal residence (ibid., pp. 338–39). Shakespeare introduces phallic violence as early as the open-ing scene in the dialogue between Sampson and Gregory and the melee that en-sues, but it continues in the confrontations between Tybalt and Romeo and between Tybalt and Mercutio.

Mercutio's volleys of sexual innuendo show his speeches to be as aggressive as fighting, and they at once establish his claim to virility while also marking his dis-tance from women. His Queen Mab speech, spectacular as it is, reveals his fear of submitting to "the seething nighttime world of unconscious desires associated with the feminine; he prefers the broad daylight world of men fighting and jest-ing" (ibid., p. 343). Later, when Romeo lies in despair in Friar Lawrence's cell be-moaning his banishment, cursing his name and wanting to sever it from himself (3.3.102–8), Kahn calls this "symbolic castration": "as a consequence of the feud he cannot happily be a man either by fighting for his name and family or by loving Juliet. Banished and apart from her, he will have no identity and nothing to live for" (ibid., p. 344). The conflict between manhood as aggression and manhood as loving a woman lies at the heart of this tragedy.

So does the opposition between Thanatos and Eros, but in the lovers' suicides, love and death merge. They may be consumed and destroyed by the feud, but they also rise above it, united in death. Like others, Kahn makes much of the womb/tomb imagery in the play, especially Romeo's recognition of the tomb where Juliet lies as a "womb of death" (5.3.45). When Friar Lawrence arrives and sees the blood-splattered entrance to the tomb, Kahn says his lines (140–41) recall "both a defloration and an initiation into sexuality, and a birth" (ibid., p. 353); she compares Juliet's earlier association of her marriage bed with her grave (1.5.134). The birth that occurs is perversely a birth into death, a return to the tomb of the fa-thers, not the birth of an adult self for which the lovers strove in vain. But that is to look at the situation only one way. Another way, following the deaths of the lovers, is to see their suicides as a rebirth into a higher stage of existence—a willed and triumphant assertion on the part of both over "the impoverished and destructive world which has kept them apart" (ibid., p. 354). The lovers thus come of age by a means different from the usual rites of passage in Verona: phallic violence and adolescent motherhood. Romeo's death in the Capulets' tomb reverses the tradi-tional passage of the female over to the male house in marriage and further beto-kens his refusal to follow the code of his fathers.[7]

More recent psychoanalytical criticism has tended to follow the theories of Jacques Lacan rather than those of Sigmund Freud. Julia Kristeva, a professor of linguistics at the University of Paris VII and one of the leading exponents of post-Lacanian psychoanalytical criticism, has written on *Romeo and Juliet* with specific reference to the theme of love/hate in the couple.[8] In her view, Romeo and Juliet spend less time loving each other than in getting ready to die (in Drakakis, ed., *Shakespearean Tragedy,* p. 298). They enjoy the frisson of a secret, forbidden love, "of being within a hairsbreadth of punishment"; from the outset their love proceeds within the shadowy presence of a third party—the feuding families. "In fact," Kristeva says, "without this third party, this commandment of the secret, the man loses his amatory submission to the threatening father. While in her avenging ardor against her own father . . . the woman recaptures with her secret lover the unsuspected jouissance of maternal fusion" (ibid., pp. 298–99). Juliet wants Romeo to doff his name, to lose his symbolic entity so that she, on the basis of his "loved fragmented body" (cp. 3.2.21–25) may become entire, whole, one. But Juliet is mistaken: Romeo's name is not irrelevant to the triggering of their passion, but determines it.

Under the guise of sex, hatred prevails, as the very first lines of the play proclaim. Juliet's most intense expressions of love show that this love is supported by hatred (ibid., p. 305). What is involved, Kristeva argues, is hatred "at the very origin of the amorous surge. A hatred that antedates the veil of amorous idealization." Juliet herself articulates the paradox: "My only love sprung from my only hate" (1.5.139). The fact remains, Kristeva says, that "Juliet's jouissance is often stated through the anticipation—the desire?—of Romeo's death" (ibid., p. 306). Kristeva thus shows the intrinsic presence of hatred within the amatory feeling. Why does Romeo so easily switch from Rosaline to Juliet? It is because both are Capulets, the same source of hatred (ibid., p. 308).

In the midst of this discussion Kristeva appears to digress to show the autobiographical relevance of Shakespeare's play, presumably written shortly after Hamnet, Shakespeare's son, died in 1596. (Recall that some psychoanalytical critics tend to be more interested in the author than in the work.) Kristeva speculates that Hamnet's death at age eleven evoked in Shakespeare "a kind of nostalgic feeling for marriage," of a couple in love "as precisely William and Anne were not able to be" (ibid., p. 304). "Against the backdrop of his own marriage made commonplace by births, branded by death," she continues, "Shakespeare, the dreamer, and already a relentless blasphemer of matriarchal-matrimonial power, sets up the dream of lovers scalded by the law of hatred but in themselves immortally sublime." *Romeo and Juliet* thus becomes "a dirge for the son's death": "The father's guilt confesses in this play, along with hatred for marriage, the desire to preserve the myth of the enamored lovers" (ibid.). The play becomes the father's gift to the son's tomb, a casting out of the son's death and an antidote, too, for a failed marriage.

Psychoanalytically oriented critics, as one might expect, have a good deal to say about Mercutio and specifically his relationship with Romeo. In *Shakespeare's Mercutio* (1988) Joseph Porter reviews and critiques much of this commentary, including studies by Janet Adelman, Marianne Novy, Kahn, and others, many of whom, Porter says, devalue Mercutio and devalue or ignore the claims of his friendship with Romeo. The rivalry between friendship and love is Shakespeare's most significant single alteration of the source story, Porter reminds us. Their conflicting claims are most open-mindedly presented in this play and transform a canonical story of heterosexual love into a story of the opposition between it and friendship (p. 154).

To what extent, then, does this friendship suggest, or even demand, a homosexual interpretation? Porter very carefully examines the evidence in detail, both in the play and intertextually, and concludes that Mercutio's references to Romeo's phallus "add up to a highly Mercurial stance combining an opposition to love, an amiable erotic permissiveness, and a phallocentrism that admits traces of homoeroticism" (*Mercutio,* p. 157).[9] In Porter's view, Mercutio is Shakespeare's means of "processing" the memory of Christopher Marlowe, particularly Marlowe's sensuality. Some of his well-known homoeroticism emerges in Mercutio's characterization, but more subtly, and one cannot extrapolate from Shakespeare's depiction of Mercutio much about the author's own homosexual desire to add to what may be derived (as some believe) from his sonnets. Porter wisely takes no stand regarding the sonnets, nor does he assume any grander claim about Shakespeare's own sexual orientation than that "he seems generally heterosexual, though far less prescriptively and possibly less exclusively so than commentators in general, and feminist and psychoanalytic commentators in particular, make him out to be" (ibid., p. 160).

Both patriarchy and homosocial desire are nonetheless prominent in Franco Zeffirelli's film version of *Romeo and Juliet,* according to Peter S. Donaldson, who adduces Zeffirelli's autobiography in support of his claims.[10] The obsessive verbal equation of erect penis and sword that Zeffirelli found in Shakespeare's text becomes translated visually in the film. The men's bodies are "objects of an engrossed, sensual appreciation" (Donaldson, *Shakespearean Films,* p. 154). As in the text, Mercutio is the most enthusiastic of the phallic jokesters, repeatedly given to emphasizing the bawdiness of his remarks with a significant gesture. As Donaldson notes, his fatal encounter with Tybalt occurs when he is cooling off waist-deep in a fountain; at "Here's my fiddlestick" (3.1.41), he thrusts his rapier point from beneath the water in the semblance of a phallus (ibid., p. 155).

By cutting allusions to rapier and sexual assault in the dialogue of others, Zeffirelli makes Mercutio's misogyny all the more prominent. In the wild and whirling way John McEnery delivers the Queen Mab speech, the misogynist content causes Mercutio's breakdown. He breaks off his speech only when he runs out of manic energy. "His final, sad '*this* is she' suggests a partial awareness," Donaldson says, "that his inventiveness and improvisation mask an identification with the (devalued) women his discourse and antics evoke. He himself is Queen Mab: she arises from his own pain and confusion" (ibid., p. 158). Romeo's response is not a reproach, but an expression of concern and compassion. The foreheads of the young men touch briefly, then Mercutio is led away by the other friends, signaling the loss of a loving connection, the severing of male bonds, which becomes the paradigm of loss and anguish in the film (ibid., p. 159). Citing Porter, Donaldson agrees that Mercutio is ambivalent, but in Zeffirelli's film, he seems not merely Romeo's friend but his former lover, cast off when Romeo opts for women.[11]

FEMINIST AND GENDER CRITICISM

The women's movement, arising in the United States partly out of the civil rights movement of the 1950s and 1960s, is largely responsible for the growth in literary studies of feminist criticism. Insofar as they attempt to understand the nature of woman and relationships between the sexes generally, feminist and gender criticism, however, also stem directly or indirectly from some aspects of psychoanalytical criticism. The practitioners of these critical approaches are not usually psychoanalysts themselves, but like other psychoanalytically oriented critics, they are often well informed about various modes of psychoanalysis, whether or not they take a specifically designated psychoanalytical approach to their subject. Freud and his perceived bias against women is of course the bête noire of these critics, who attempt to found a more evenhanded critique of sexuality and gender relations.

Patriarchy is the other and older nemesis. Much of feminist criticism is directed against patriarchal structures in literature as in life—against, that is, male domination of the female. Recent scholarship has shown, however, that in the early modern period—the period of *Romeo and Juliet*—the situation was more complicated than a simple, reductionist view of patriarchy would make it appear. Women had their own ways of challenging male authority, then as now.[12] Ann More, who secretly married John Donne, is just one example testifying to this fact in real life, just as Juliet and Desdemona among others in Elizabethan and Jacobean drama testify to it in literature.

In the introduction to one of the first anthologies of feminist criticism, *The Woman's Part* (1980), the editors begin by attempting to define their subject. Feminist criticism, they say, "pays acute attention to the woman's part in literature. But it is not only and not always feminocentric, for it examines both men and women and the social structures that shape them."[13] Such criticism may be written by men as well as women, for feminist criticism "is more a matter of perspective than of subject matter or gender. Feminists assume that women are equal to men but that their roles . . . have been restricted, stereotyped, and minimized; their aim is to free women from oppressive restraints."[14] Twenty years later, much of this agenda has been accomplished, though much remains. Moreover, gender studies—with or without a particular point of view—have also become important. Feminist and gender criticism together have opened new avenues of research and understanding in Shakespeare studies, as they have done in many areas of literary and other endeavors.

Not surprisingly, Kahn's essay "On Coming of Age in Verona" is included in *The Woman's Part,* partly because of its treatment of male aggression and the despotic patriarchy represented by the Capulets and Montagues. In another, more widely ranging but also psychoanalytically influenced essay, " 'I Wooed Thee with

My Sword': Shakespeare's Tragic Paradigms," Madelon Gohlke analyzes the metaphor in her title, noting the equivalence of the sword to the phallus. In *A Midsummer Night's Dream,* from which the line comes, love may be either generated or secured by hostility, she says, and Theseus and Hippolyta take up sadistic and masochistic postures in relation to each other, attitudes that reverberate elsewhere throughout the play.[15] To participate in the masculine ethic of *Romeo and Juliet* is to participate in the feud, as the opening lines strikingly indicate. From Sampson's words it is clear that the feud defines men as intensely competitive and their relations with women as controlling and violent. Romeo initially appears to reject this ethic, but his relationship with Juliet "anticipates and ultimately incorporates violence" (Gohlke, " 'I Wooed Thee,' " p. 152). Romeo seeks danger by wooing Juliet and death by threatening suicide after he kills Tybalt; Juliet, too, threatens suicide when she first hears the news of Tybalt's death at Romeo's hands. "Read metaphorically," Gohlke says, "the plot validates the perception expressed variously in the play that love kills" (ibid., p. 153).

In her chapter "Violence, Love, and Gender" in *Love's Argument* (1984), Marianne Novy also discusses violence with particular reference to the blood feud engendered by patriarchal structures in *Romeo and Juliet.* If in their private world the young lovers are able to establish a mutuality in love that transcends conventional roles, this world is destroyed by Romeo's entanglement in the feud.[16] It matters little, ultimately, that Romeo ceases using conventional images of love's siege for more benign ones after he meets Juliet, that he is willing to surrender his very name for love of her. His shifting idiom in no way signifies a diminution of sexual energy and attraction, which Juliet shares as or more intensely. Although both use the language of trade and property, they do so in a way that does not suggest female social subordination or purely financial interest, as exemplified in Lady Capulet's praise of Paris. Nevertheless, Novy says, "the asymmetry in their use of financial imagery coheres with the asymmetrical demands that the male code of violence will make on Romeo and the female code of docility on Juliet" (*Love's Argument,* p. 105).

Novy also questions why Romeo keeps his love of Juliet a secret from others, especially Benvolio and Mercutio. She says that by excluding Mercutio from his confidence, Romeo challenges not only the feud but also the associations of masculinity and sexuality with violence, but to no avail (ibid., p. 106). After Tybalt kills Mercutio under his arm, Romeo feels compelled to take revenge for his friend's death, deploring as he does so that Juliet's beauty has made him "effeminate" (3.1.112). To this extent, he is still bound by Verona's code of violence. Similarly, Juliet is forced to yield to gender constraints when she accedes to the Friar's counsel and pretends submission to her parents' demands to marry Paris, even though she is willing to commit suicide rather than betray Romeo. Novy concludes that by making Romeo and Juliet mere teenagers, Shakespeare emphasized their inexperience and innocence. Their extreme purity gives their love its special tragedy, as many audiences have acknowledged. "The play expresses both the appeal and the danger of a love in which two people become the whole world to each other" (ibid., p. 109). Only through their deaths can the lovers negotiate a recognition by the outer world and its gender ideals.[17]

Dympna Callaghan's goal in "The Ideology of Romantic Love: The Case of *Romeo and Juliet*" is to examine the play and its role in the cultural construction of desire, which, she claims, are highly significant for feminist studies. This is because, in its most common formulation as transhistorical romantic love, desire "is one of the most efficient and irresistible interpellations of the female subject, securing her complicity in apparently unchangeable structures of oppression, particularly compulsory heterosexuality and bourgeois marriage."[18] The ideology of romantic love from the Renaissance onward centers on women's subjective experience, Callaghan says, but this focus tends to control and delimit intimate experience rather than allowing the fullest expression of female desire. She therefore proceeds to analyze the ideological function of *Romeo and Juliet* in the Renaissance and the present and then to critique psychoanalytical and historical discourses that actually impede the historicization of desire in Renaissance studies rather than enable it, as they should.

Shakespeare's text has perpetuated the dominant ideology of romantic love and enacts the propensity to posit desire as transhistorical, that is, not limited to a single era or epoch. According to Kristeva and others, the play conveys a universal legend of love representing elemental psychic forces of desire and frustration common to every age and culture. But is this legend accurate or true historically? Replication of the play in editions and performances (to say nothing of critical analyses) helps to substantiate and confirm the legend, Callaghan argues, and makes it resistant to historicization. But, in fact, the play's inclination toward replication and multiplication is basically "a maneuver that propagates a version of erotic love which is consonant with the needs of an emergent social order" ("Ideology of Romantic Love," p. 62). Later in her essay Callaghan describes that social order and, using mainly Marxist analysis, explains how it came into being, that is, how *Romeo and Juliet* consolidated the ideology of romantic love and the correlative crystallization of the modern nuclear family.

The cultural production of desire, in which the play participates, was required by the rise of absolutism, the centralization of the state, and the advent of capitalism (ibid., p. 71). As Callaghan shows in her analysis of the role of Prince Escalus, whom she considers the pivotal character in the play, *Romeo and Juliet* dramatizes the shift from family allegiances associated with feudalism to those identified with centralization of the state. Put another way, "the *shifting configurations* of patriarchal law and the changing formations of desire which attend it comprise the structure and substance of Shakespeare's text" (ibid., p. 72). As power transfers from the feuding fathers to the Prince, the play articulates a crisis in patriarchy itself. But although *Romeo and Juliet* is completely coincident with the dominant ideology of desire, multiple and contradictory discourses of the desire are also negotiated in the isolation and idealization of romantic heterosexual love. As Mercutio's Queen Mab speech shows, the disembodied libido can take many and various courses, from the sexual desires of women to the greed and blood lust of men.

Mercutio thereby articulates the plasticity of desire, which is "both controlled and aberrant, chaotic—its objective is either death or reproduction" (ibid., p. 73).

Romeo and Juliet made its cultural intervention at a time when the ideology of love and marriage and the organization of desire to sustain it were undergoing change. The change was the result of the Puritan doctrine of marriage, which was imbued with idealism and stressed less the evils of female sexuality and more the benefits of pliant sexuality than earlier writings had done (ibid., p. 79). Women were endowed with desiring subjectivity, which could then be actively solicited and controlled by the social order. Enforced marriage (such as Capulet attempts to impose on Juliet in his arrangement with Paris) gave way to the concept of freely circulating love. At a crucial moment in the garden scene (2.2.89–101) Juliet ceases to engage in elaborate negotiations and exchanges of erotic power that constitute courtship, because the play is not about power within the couple, but about the power relation between the lovers and the outside world (ibid., p. 81). On the other hand, Romeo and Juliet's love could have provided the diplomatic solution to the feud, as Friar Lawrence had hoped; while it offers resistance to the feudal households, it is perfectly compatible with the interests of society as a whole. "Thus, the utopian, dangerous, and paradoxical notion of a law that ratifies (inherently transgressive) passion, becomes the desideratum of early modern marriage" (ibid., p. 86). In sum, *Romeo and Juliet* addresses some of the contradictions of post-Reformation patriarchy, for example, the attempt to produce the authority of husbands, fathers, and magistrates (the state) as mutually reinforcing, while at the same time supporting the effort to appropriate the transgressive aspects of desire (ibid., p. 87). As marriage was increasingly sanctified, so, too, were the figures of authority. Although *Romeo and Juliet* stands as an apparently "benign, lyrical document of universal love," it does not stand above history, but rather within it, as Callaghan shows, "doing the work of culture, instigating and perpetuating the production of socially necessary formations of desire" (ibid., p. 88).

Feminist and gender criticism have focused not only on the nature of woman, but also on masculinity, as Robert Appelbaum has done in " 'Standing to the wall': The Pressures of Masculinity in *Romeo and Juliet*."[19] The question of masculinity is peculiarly relevant to this play, as some of the previous discussion has shown. The opening dialogue between Sampson and Gregory implicitly raises it, as does Friar Lawrence later, quite explicitly, regarding Romeo's behavior ("Art thou a man?" 3.3.110–35). Appelbaum argues that here as elsewhere in Shakespeare "masculinity seems to have a doubleness that is all but insoluble" (p. 252). Against the opening and recurring spectacle of masculine aggression, *Romeo and Juliet* juxtaposes a pair of alternatives: civil peace, as proclaimed by Prince Escalus, and civil love, as exemplified by the young lovers and the regime of heterosexual love they try to observe, albeit secretly. But in Appelbaum's view, these are not genuine alternatives, because the masculinity is constituted as a system from which there is neither any escape nor any experience of masculine satisfaction (" 'Standing to the Wall,' " p. 253).

Appelbaum recognizes that in the current state of critical theory masculinity is always at fault:

> Masculinity isn't innocent. It is a structure, a regime, a dominant system that is held to account; and what it is held to account for is the violence and oppression that seems [sic] to be the corollary of its hegemony. Whatever else it may be, masculinity is the gender of destructive aggression on the one hand and of homosocial domination on the other. (Ibid., pp. 256–57)

He therefore tries to conceptualize a "healthy masculinity," one worth achieving despite the difficulties presented by the present critical climate in which masculinity as such is suspect and marked as pathological, even as it is assumed to be "normative, inescapable, and indispensable" (ibid., p. 258).

The polarity in the very concept of gender contributes to this problem. To be a man is not to be a woman; to be a woman is to be one of those weaklings forced against the wall by men, who are always already hegemonic. Or, in other words, not being a woman means being a subject complicit in the domination of women. Is there any way out of this catch-22? Only by overcoming relationality, it seems:

> If masculinity is a quality or family of qualities that acquires its meaning from relationality with respect to femininity, it is also a relational condition that aspires to efface its relationality, to raise itself to a condition of self-adequacy, where the category of femininity is moot. . . . The manliness that Friar Lawrence wants Romeo to exemplify is a condition of self-directedness and self-control: it is not only a way of not being a woman; it is also a way of not being a lower animal. (Ibid., p. 261)

But even this apparently healthy masculinity that Friar Lawrence urges may also be the work of an oppressive ideology. It may be possible, however, to bypass both the repudiating and the pathologizing of masculinity as it exists in Shakespeare and to grant that in plays like *Romeo and Juliet* men seldom, if ever, attain the goal of normative masculinity that is the ideological justification for the oppression of women. It may be possible, then, to see men as *"failing subjects,* whose failure is *also* a part of the regime of masculinity and its ideological norms, but whose failure is precisely what makes them . . . into the subjects whose ethical dilemmas and psychic dramas are of interest to us" (ibid., p. 262). Appelbaum cites Capulet, Montague, and Friar Lawrence as versions of failed paternalism or imperfect masculinities, tied together in Verona's fundamentally stable social structure, whose absolute legality is embodied in Prince Escalus (ibid., pp. 266–68). And if the fathers are ineffectual, the sons are self-destructive. What Appelbaum finds crucial is that against the norms represented by the Prince and the citizens—Verona's adequate masculine legality—the play juxtaposes "the inward experience of failed normativity and represents this failure as the structure of life among its tragic men" (ibid., p. 268). The men we come to know are all under pressure to perform, but to perform as imperatives to achieve the impossible, to end a cycle of repetition by repetition.

The alternative of erotic desire and its accompanying pacifism, represented by Romeo, is likewise compromised by the inadequate masculinity of the feuding fathers. The erotic drive also seems to place men in a condition of indeterminate satisfaction, according to Appelbaum, even as it is a fundamental condition of the performance of masculinity. After he meets Juliet, Romeo tries to "deploy desire's conventionality as a pretext not for escaping the imperatives of masculine aggression, as he earlier tried to do, but for turning them into the imperatives of the symbolic order itself, imperatives that among other things demand the resolution of the family feud and all the masculine inadequacies that have sustained it" (ibid., p. 270). When he intervenes, however, in the conflict between Mercutio and Tybalt, he is unable merely by invoking the law to cause it to be observed, since he lacks the sovereign authority that only the Prince possesses.

Thus Romeo, seduced into thinking he can escape the system by sublimating aggression into law, is instead transformed into a more perfect representative of the regime of masculinity and its masks. When he hears of Juliet's burial and assumes she is dead, he finds the solution to the dilemma of masculinity, Appelbaum claims, by refusing either to stir or to stand; "he'll fulfill his masculinist calling by lying down, sacrificing himself. And, as the play makes clear, the social order will be much the better for it" (ibid., p. 271). In death, Romeo fulfills the highest ideals of the social order, of civil love and civil peace. But he does not accomplish those ideals for his self. Although he cannot do without it, the regime of masculine performance has always been separating from Romeo, and ending that separation—the goal, perhaps, and reward of erotic love—is possible only in death. As Shakespearean tragedy is the tragedy of men, it is the tragedy of masculine performance, of inevitable inadequacies that nevertheless determine the drama of social and political order in the Shakespearean universe. The full masculinity that few, if any, can attain—unimpaired legality and force—is nonetheless a principle of order that men cannot do without, however much they may try to escape its consequences in trying to make themselves, like Romeo, into subjects trying to be men.

MYTH AND ARCHETYPAL CRITICISM

One of the earliest advocates and practitioners of myth and archetypal criticism was Maud Bodkin, whose *Archetypal Patterns in Poetry: Psychological Studies of the Imagination* (1934) drew upon the theories of Carl Jung and Gilbert Murray. She studied the way that certain themes, especially in tragedy, showed a persistence with the life of a community or race and compared the different forms they assumed. More recently, Northrop Frye developed the approach in "Archetypal Criticism: Theory of Myths," the third chapter of his monumental work, *Anatomy of Criticism* (1957). He begins his study of archetypes with the world of myth, which he defines as "an abstract or purely literary world of fictional and thematic design, unaffected by canons of plausible adaptation to familiar experience." The meaning or pattern of poetry is "a structure of imagery with conceptional implications."[20] It is these patterns that archetypal criticism attempts to identify and explain.

In Chapter 6 on themes in *Romeo and Juliet,* the *Liebestod* (love-death) myth and Shakespeare's divergence from it have already been briefly addressed. In *The Stranger in Shakespeare,* Leslie Fiedler recalls another ancient, related myth, which he traces back to Ovid's *Metamorphoses*: the legend of Pyramus and Thisbe. We know that Ovid was Shakespeare's favorite classical poet, and while he travesties the Pyramus and Thisbe story in *A Midsummer Night's Dream,* he treats it far more seriously in *Romeo and Juliet.* The myth has its origins (so far as anyone knows) in the belief that those who defy their fathers, even in love's name, deserve to die. Pyramus and Thisbe, separated by their parents, nevertheless fall in love and plan to run away from their homes together. While Thisbe awaits her lover at Ninus's tomb, a lioness, her jaws crimsoned from feeding on her prey, scares the young woman away and then tears her dropped veil to pieces. When Pyramus arrives and sees the animal's tracks and the bloody veil, he concludes that Thisbe is dead and commits suicide, his spurting blood staining forever the berries on the mulberry tree under which Thisbe had waited for him. Afraid of disappointing her lover, Thisbe comes out of hiding and returns to find Pyramus dying. She follows him in death, her warm blood mingling with his, but not before she prays that her parents will understand and bury her together with Pyramus and that the gods will retain in the mulberries their new dark and mournful color as a remembrance of their deaths.[21]

The myth, according to Fiedler, obsessed Shakespeare throughout the early part of his career, for he refers to it in plays such as *Titus Andronicus* and *The Merchant of Venice,* as well as *A Midsummer Night's Dream.* Those who worry much over why Romeo and Juliet have to die do not understand or appreciate the myth sufficiently. Ovid understood it and so did his Elizabethan "alter ego," Shakespeare. It is the myth that kills Romeo and Juliet, the myth that "insists . . . that every marriage makes a father weep and that for those tears the price is blood." Later, in *The Merchant of Venice,* Shakespeare seems to exorcise that archetypal ghost by substituting for Ovid's bloody fable the happy-ending folktale of the ogre's daughter.[22]

In "Shakespeare, Hypnos, and Thanatos: *Romeo and Juliet* in the Space of Myth," Jean-Marie Maguin traces the elements of several myths, or archetypes, reflected in Shakespeare's play. The first is the myth of Thanatos (Death) and his younger brother, Hypnos (Sleep), the two fatherless sons of Nyx (Night). But in a "rhetorically trained mind," such as Shakespeare's, Sleep becomes through wishful thinking the elder brother and the model; death is nothing other than the ultimate form of sleep, a sleep eternal.[23] But in *Romeo and Juliet,* Friar Lawrence constructs a hybrid, "Hypthanatos," the trance that Juliet falls into after she drinks the potion he gives her. This rival to the brothers Hypnos and Thanatos, a product of the Friar's overreaching, defies nature. As a result, he and the charges under his care must suffer. (In his later plays, Shakespeare relaxes the tension between Hypnos and Thanatos, and the desired inversion mentioned above is fulfilled, as in *Cymbeline* and *The Winter's Tale*.)

Shakespeare may also have drawn upon the myth of Cupid and Psyche, as recounted in the second century by Apuleius in *The Golden Ass*. In this myth Psyche is a king's daughter whose beauty frightens men away. She therefore is unable to find a husband and becomes a cult figure for whom people desert the altars of Aphrodite. She is finally taken away and abandoned on a mountaintop, where a dreadful monster supposedly will come for her. Instead, she finds herself in the garden of a beautiful palace, and at night her mysterious husband comes and lies with her. She is warned that she may not see him, but one night she conceals a lamp in her chamber. She lights it when her husband is asleep and sees that he is none other than Cupid, the god of love. Amazed, she lets a drop of hot oil from the lamp fall on the sleeper, who awakens and, as he had threatened, deserts her. Heartbroken, Psyche wanders, pursued by the wrath of jealous Aphrodite, who subjects her to various ordeals. The last of these involves bringing back from Hades a bottle of precious springwater that she is by no means to open. Once again she disobeys and is immediately overcome by a deathlike sleep. Meanwhile, Cupid, also heartbroken, gains permission from Zeus to marry Psyche. He awakens her by pricking her with one of his arrows; she becomes reconciled with Aphrodite, drinks ambrosia, and becomes immortal. She and Cupid have a daughter named Pleasure.[24]

In Psyche's recurrent episodes of despair, during which she is tempted to commit suicide (in Apuleius's account), as well as in her deathlike trance, Maguin finds analogues to Shakespeare's *Romeo and Juliet*. Romeo's nighttime consummation with Juliet and his flight at daybreak in 3.5 is also analogous to Cupid's experience with Psyche. Modern renditions of myth often involve inversions of some kind; Shakespeare transfers the magic power of beauty over light to Juliet when Romeo first lays eyes on her (1.5.43) and again later when he sees her in the tomb (5.3.85–86). Similarly, while Psyche is forbidden to open the vial of water, Juliet is urged to drink off Friar Lawrence's potion, but the result is the same: both fall into a deathlike trance.[25]

The main difference between the myth and Shakespeare's play is that the first ends well, whereas the second ends tragically. This ending suggests yet another inversion of myth or legend: the tale of Prince Charming and Sleeping Beauty. In Shakespeare's play one arrives too early and the other awakens too late.[26] Why Shakespeare chose to alter myth in these ways we may never know. But as Frye says, "Anyone accustomed to think archetypally of literature will recognize in tragedy a mimesis of sacrifice."[27] Furthermore, "As a mimesis of ritual, the tragic hero is not really killed or eaten, but the corresponding thing in art still takes place, a vision of death which draws the survivors into a new unity."[28] At the end of *Romeo and Juliet,* in the handclasp of Montague and Capulet, we see something of that new unity brought about by the sacrificial deaths of the two lovers.

NOTES

1. Norman N. Holland, *Psychoanalysis and Shakespeare* (New York: McGraw-Hill, 1966), pp. 4–5.

2. For an excellent discussion of the problems of applying psychoanalytical methods to literary criticism, especially when dealing with early modern texts, see Meredith Skura, "Understanding the Living and Talking to the Dead: The Historicity of Psychoanalysis," *Modern Language Quarterly* 54 (1993): 77–89. Although, as she says, "no form of indirect analysis is as useful as the results of prolonged clinical exchanges" (p. 77), she believes much can be gained by examining texts and looking for "patterns of repetition and inconsistency," for the "royal road to subjectivity in any context is texts" (p. 89).

3. Quoted by Holland, *Psychoanalysis*, p. 22.

4. "Freud was a psychologist, not a critic," Holland reminds us, and the "real aim" of his inquiry was the mind of the artist (ibid., p. 25). He repeats the first point at the beginning of his chapter titled "Freud on Shakespeare" (p. 55) and further states that Freud's primary interest was the "mind of man." Freud used Shakespeare's insights mainly to confirm his own.

5. Holland (ibid., pp. 264–67) summarizes Meninger's views and those of others mentioned in this section unless otherwise noted.

6. Coppélia Kahn, "Coming of Age in Verona," originally published in *Modern Language Studies* 8 (1978): 171–93; reprinted in John F. Andrews, ed., *"Romeo and Juliet": Critical Essays* (New York: Garland, 1993), pp. 337–58. References are to the reprint.

7. See also Marjorie Garber, *Coming of Age in Shakespeare* (London: Methuen, 1981), pp. 165–70, esp. pp. 168–70, who compares the Romeo and Juliet story with the myth of Cupid and Psyche, which (in Erich Neumann's words) exemplifies the phenomenon of love as stronger than death and, anointed with divine beauty, is willing to receive the beloved as the bridegroom of death. See the discussion of this myth in the section "Myth and Archetypal Criticism" below.

8. Her essay is reprinted from Julia Kristeva, *Tales of Love*, trans. Leon S. Roudiez (New York: Columbia University Press, 1987), pp. 209–33, in *Shakespearean Tragedy*, ed. John Drakakis (London: Longman, 1992), pp. 297–315. References are to the reprint.

9. Jonathan Goldberg follows Porter here but not to the extent that he assumes homoerotic desire must operate "within the regimes of a closet text." The boundaries for such desire, Goldberg argues, were more fluid in Shakespeare's time, and thus there is no need, he says, to make them unavailable, which locating homoeroticism as subliminal does. See *"Romeo and Juliet's* Open Rs," in *Queering the Renaissance,* ed. Jonathan Goldberg (Durham, N.C.: Duke University Press, 1994), pp. 219–35, esp. p. 235 n. 12; reprinted in *Critical Essays on "Romeo and Juliet,"* ed. Joseph A. Porter (New York: G. K. Hall, 1997), pp. 82–96.

10. Peter S. Donaldson, *Shakespearean Films/Shakespearean Directors* (Boston: Unwin Hyman, 1990), pp. 145–88.

11. Cp. Bruce Smith, *Homosexual Desire in Shakespeare's England* (Chicago: University of Chicago Press, 1991), p. 64: "An exemplar of male violence and misogyny? A martyr to male friendship? A victim of sexual desire that he cannot, will not, or must not acknowledge directly? Mercutio is all three."

12. See Juliet Dusinberre, *Shakespeare and the Nature of Women*, 2nd ed. (New York: St. Martin's Press, 1996), p. xvii. Dusinberre's preface to the second edition, published twenty years after the first, surveys the development of feminist criticism, especially but not exclusively related to Shakespeare study.

13. *The Woman's Part: Feminist Criticism of Shakespeare,* ed. Carolyn Ruth Swift Lenz, Gayle Greene, and Carol Thomas Neely (Urbana: University of Illinois Press, 1980), p. 3.

14. Ibid.

15. Madelon Gohlke, " 'I Wooed Thee with My Sword': Shakespeare's Tragic Paradigms," in *The Woman's Part,* ed. Lenz et al., p. 151.

16. Marianne Novy, *Love's Argument: Gender Relations in Shakespeare* (Chapel Hill: University of North Carolina Press, 1984), p. 100. See also Kiernan Ryan, "*Romeo and Juliet*: The Language of Tragedy," in *The Taming of the Text,* ed. Willie Van Peer (London: Routledge, 1988), pp. 107–21. The "utopian quality" of Romeo and Juliet's love, Ryan says, is stressed from the start of act 2. "Its subversive implications proceed from the fact that it is founded on equality and reciprocity rather than subservience" (p. 117).

17. Cp. Ryan, "Language of Tragedy": The source of the play's power lies "in the way the lovers come to embody the possibility of a more satisfying form of sexual relationship, free of the social and ideological constraints which continue to divide men and women from each other and prevent the full and equal realization of mutual desire" (pp. 109–10).

18. Dympna C. Callaghan, "The Ideology of Romantic Love: The Case of *Romeo and Juliet,*" in Dympna C. Callaghan, Lorraine Helms, and Jyotsna Singh, *The Weyward Sisters: Shakespeare and Feminist Politics* (Oxford: Blackwell, 1994), pp. 59–60.

19. Robert Appelbaum, " 'Standing to the Wall': The Pressures of Masculinity in *Romeo and Juliet,*" *Shakespeare Quarterly* 48 (1997): 251–72.

20. Northrop Frye, *Anatomy of Criticism* (Princeton, N.J.: Princeton University Press, 1957), p. 136.

21. Ovid, *Metamorphoses,* trans. Rolfe Humphries (Bloomington: University of Indiana Press, 1957), pp. 83–86. In his lecture on *Romeo and Juliet,* Northrop Frye says that no story was more loved or frequently retold in Shakespeare's day than that of Pyramus and Thisbe; moreover, at the same time and on the other side of the world, Chikamatsu, the Japanese writer of Bunraku, or puppet plays, was telling similar stories. The myth is far older than even Ovid's tales. See *Frye on Shakespeare,* ed. Robert Sandler (New Haven, Conn.: Yale University Press, 1986), p. 30.

22. Leslie Fiedler, *The Stranger in Shakespeare* (New York: Stein and Day, 1972), pp. 128–29. For his discussion of the ogre's daughter, who betrays her inhuman father and steals his treasure for the sake of a human hero, see pp. 111–12.

23. Jean-Marie Maguin, "Shakespeare, Hypnos, and Thanatos: *Romeo and Juliet* in the Space of Myth," in *"Romeo and Juliet": Texts, Contexts, and Interpretation,* ed. Jay L. Halio (Newark: University of Delaware Press, 1995), p. 37. Maguin cites *The Tempest* (4.1.156–58), specifically, Prospero's comparison of life and dreams, death and sleep.

24. This account is drawn from Maguin's summary, ibid., pp. 41–42. For a more detailed account, see *Bulfinch's Mythology* (New York: Modern Library, n.d.), pp. 68–77. In Bulfinch's account, it is not a bottle of springwater but a box containing some of Proserpine's beauty that Psyche must carry back to Aphrodite.

25. Maguin, "Shakespeare, Hypnos, and Thantos," pp. 42–43.

26. Ibid., p. 47.

27. Frye, *Anatomy of Criticism,* p. 214. This approach, however, seems to have fallen out of favor, at least among American scholars, who apparently prefer to study the ritual aspects of drama only. See, for example, Linda Woodbridge's introduction to *True Rites and Maimed Rites: Ritual and Anti-Ritual in Shakespeare and His Age* (Urbana: University of Illinois Press, 1992), pp. 1–43.

28. Frye, ibid., p. 215.

THE PLAY IN PERFORMANCE

ELIZABETHAN AND SEVENTEENTH-CENTURY PRODUCTIONS

Of the first performances of Shakespeare's *Romeo and Juliet* we know little or nothing, although the evidence of publication indicates that, from the beginning, it must have been a popular play. The title page of the first quarto says that "it hath been often (with great applause) plaid publiquely," and the title page of Q2 states that "it hath bene sundry times publiquely acted." The two quartos, followed by others in 1609 and 1622, also attest to its popularity, but we have no record of an actual performance until after the Restoration in 1660. Ironically, as G. B. Evans notes in the *New Cambridge Shakespeare* (pp. 28–29), we know more about performances on the continent of Europe than we do about those in England, since the play was included in the repertoire of groups known as the "English Comedians," who toured with German or Dutch versions. Nevertheless, from other evidence we can infer some information regarding Shakespeare's play in late sixteenth-century England.

The company that first produced the play in England was composed of members from other London companies who were disbanding, such as the Queen's Men. The new company was called the Lord Chamberlain's Men, since it came under the patronage and protection of the Lord Chamberlain, Henry Carey, and then his son, George.[1] Will Kemp was certainly the actor who played Peter (and probably the Clown, or Servant, in 1.2 as well): Q2 actually names Kemp instead of Peter in the stage direction at 4.5.99. Richard Burbage, as the company's leading actor, was very likely the first Romeo and Master Robert Goffe the first Juliet. Possibly, Thomas Pope played Mercutio, Shakespeare Prince Escalus, and William Sly Tybalt. John Heminges and Henry Condell, who later collected Shakespeare's plays for the First Folio, may have played Old Capulet and Paris, respectively.[2] According to T. J. King's computations, the Q1 version of the play would have required nine men and three boys for the principal parts, with an additional seven men and two boys for minor roles, including doubling of parts. The Q2 version would have required more principal actors, fourteen in all, and twice as many as Q1 for minor roles—eighteen, including doubling (although of these eighteen, nine were merely supers, or walk-ons, who had no speaking parts).[3]

In the mid-1590s, the Lord Chamberlain's Men performed at various theaters, including The Curtain and The Theatre, London's first theaters.[4] These theaters, modeled after bearbaiting rings, were large amphitheaters that could hold as many as 2,500 spectators. For a penny, one gained admission to the yard; for another penny, one could get a seat in the tiered, covered galleries. Performances took place in the afternoons during daylight hours, and those who stood in the yard on three sides of the raised platform stage, partly covered by a canopy, or "heavens," were in close proximity to the actors. These so-called groundlings enjoyed greater intimacy with the actors and the action than those seated in the galleries and much more than is possible in modern proscenium stage, or picture-frame, theaters.[5] The action moved swiftly, actors coming on stage from one of the two stage doors in the rear wall as those in the previous scene left by the other door. Plays, which lasted roughly two hours, as the Prologue to *Romeo and Juliet* indicates, were performed without intervals.

Just when and where the premiere of *Romeo and Juliet* was staged we do not know. Some evidence suggests that it was played for a time at The Curtain, since The Theatre (which James Burbage, Richard's father, owned) remained dark during 1597–1598. Thomas Marston apparently alludes to a performance there in his satire *Scourge of Villainy* (1598).[6] After 1599, revivals would have occurred at the Globe, which was built that year from the timbers of the old Theatre and became the London home for the company. After 1609, when the King's Men could at last perform in their "private" theater in the City at Blackfriars, performances were indoors and lit by candlelight.

Staging in the Elizabethan theater was not a highly complicated affair, since the accoutrements of the modern theater were unknown. On an essentially bare stage, the actors depended more upon language and gesture than upon sets and other stage decoration. Not that props were entirely unavailable. In *Romeo and Juliet,* swords, fans, a rope ladder for Romeo in 3.5, a bed for Juliet in 4.3–5, and other props were required, to say nothing of the tomb in which she and Tybalt were placed and which was in view during the last scene. What the stage lacked in decoration, notwithstanding the painted cloths that hung over the rear wall, it made up for in rich and elaborate costumes.[7] Music, too, was available and called for in two scenes, 1.5 and 4.5. In the second of these scenes, the musicians actually appear on stage and in dialogue with Peter; in the first, they may have occupied a gallery space above the stage proper used by them in this play and in others.

Although many plays required only one level for performance, the garden and balcony scenes in *Romeo and Juliet* (2.2 and 3.5) obviously required some kind of "above." Q1 is useful in providing many stage directions absent in Q2 that help us visualize staging in early productions, but the dialogue, too, offers direction. In

3.5, the initial stage direction in Q1 reads "*Enter Romeo and Iuliet at the window*";
in Q2, "*Enter* Romeo *and* Iuliet *aloft*." Many modern editions, for example, the
New Arden, combine these directions, indicating that Q1's "window" is located
above the main stage in this scene and presumably (though the quartos are silent
there) also in 2.2, which requires a similar configuration for the action. What complicates the movement in the portmanteau scene, 3.5, is that after Romeo "goes
down" (l. 42), as Q1 directs, and then off, Juliet also must descend later at line 67,
as Q1 also directs, to meet her mother, who calls her from below. Juliet does this
in the short space of a very few lines. The rest of the scene takes place on the main
stage, where of course it would have to do so, since Capulet and the Nurse join the
action later (l. 125). There would scarcely be room for all four in the restricted
space "aloft."[8]

Since the Elizabethan stage was basically nonillusionist, a scene could represent
any place designated by the dialogue or no specific location at all. Productions did
not require the kind of scene shifts that have become commonplace on the modern
stage. A change of scene and a change of place occurred simultaneously and immediately, a practice that helped speed up the action—unlike the cumbersome
stagings introduced in Victorian productions that often required long intervals to
put new scenery in place. Hence, in 1.4–5, for example, the action moves quickly
and easily from the street outdoors to the ball inside the Capulet house. Similarly,
2.1–2 moves from outside the garden wall to inside the garden, where Romeo
catches a glimpse of Juliet on her balcony.

Staging the tomb scene is a more complex matter. Here the inner stage (or "discovery space," as it is now called), covered with a traverse curtain and located
under the gallery between the two stage doors, becomes important, as it does also
in 4.3, where Juliet's bed is thrust out from within. In 5.3, the same space must
have been used to display the bodies of Tybalt and Juliet, although this portmanteau scene begins outside the tomb, where Paris first appears to strew flowers and
then duels with Romeo. After disposing of Paris, Romeo forces open the tomb
with the mattock and "crow" he has asked Balthasar to bring him. If the tomb is
the curtained discovery space, he would just mime the strenuous action of forcing
open the tomb. Or perhaps, as Evans speculates, framed wooden doors were
slipped across the discovery space for a more realistic representation.[9] Alterna-
tively, Romeo might have pried open the lid of the trapdoor in front of the discovery space, turned to face Paris, and then opened the curtain to discover the bodies
of Tybalt and Juliet.[10] Until he leaves to call the Watch, Paris's page could have
hidden behind one of the pillars holding up the stage canopy, and Balthasar could
have remained behind the other. As the scene continued, Friar Lawrence entered
from one stage door, the Watch from the other, and so on to the end. Thus, all of
the action in the scene, which involves several different though adjacent locations
on the large platform stage—the churchyard, the entrance to the tomb, the tomb itself—could occur in front of the audience without any scene breaks needed to
mount different scenery. Elizabethan staging was both fluid and flexible, to say the
least. Or, as Jill Levenson summarizes:

the continual shifts in *Romeo and Juliet*—from public to private action, from the everyday to the transcendent—occurred again and again in the same unlocalised space. . . . So the play's internal dynamic . . . became not only audible but visible and physical, its vigour conveyed in the actors' unimpeded and intense execution.[11]

RESTORATION AND EIGHTEENTH-CENTURY PRODUCTIONS

On December 12, 1660, William Davenant was granted a warrant to act *Romeo and Juliet* along with a number of other Shakespeare plays and several by Shakespeare's contemporaries. His company, the Duke's Men, revived the play in March 1662, with Henry Harris as Romeo, Thomas Betterton as Mercutio, and Mrs. Sanderson as Juliet (probably the first woman to enact the role on the professional stage).[12] Samuel Pepys saw a performance and was mightily dissatisfied: "it is the play of itself the worst that ever I heard in my life, and the worst acted that ever I saw these people do," he wrote in his *Diary*. He had paid extra to see the first performance and resolved never to go to a premiere again.[13] According to the prompter, John Downes, soon afterward James Howard transformed the play into a tragicomedy in which Romeo and Juliet did not die at the end.[14] This version was played alternately with the tragedy "several Days together," but no other account of performances is extant.

That anyone would transform *Romeo and Juliet* into a tragicomedy or otherwise substantially alter a Shakespeare play may surprise those unaware of the practice of the times. But just as Shakespeare himself rewrote old plays, so did his successors feel free to rewrite his, as indeed Thomas Otway did quite radically in the play he renamed *The Rise and Fall of Caius Marius,* performed by the Duke's Men in October 1679. Choosing to mingle Roman intrigue with Renaissance tragedy, Otway provided what Hazelton Spencer has called "the most absurdly incongruous of all Restoration versions" of Shakespeare's plays.[15] First published in 1680, Otway's redaction went through several more editions (1692, 1696, 1703). Its frequent revivals on the stage until 1727 (its last recorded performances were in 1735)[16] attest to the play's popularity and the public's taste. As an example of the way Otway rewrote Shakespeare's, consider these lines from the Queen Mab speech:[17]

Oh! the small Queen of Fairies
Is busy in his Brains; the Mab that comes,
Drawn by a little Team of smallest Atoms
Over mens Noses as they lie asleep,
In a Chariot of an empty Hazel-nut
Made by a Joiner Squirrel: in which state
She gallops night by night through Lovers brains.

In 1744, Theophilus Cibber adapted Shakespeare's *Romeo and Juliet.* Though he incorporated passages from Otway and a similar death scene, his version did not achieve the same popularity.

Two years later, in 1746, Thomas Sheridan also adapted Shakespeare's play and had a successful run at Smock Alley, Dublin. Although this adaptation failed to become the hit that Otway's had been, it, along with Cibber's, probably inspired David Garrick's version, which, in 1748, began the longest run of the play in its history.[18] From the initial performance at Drury Lane until 1776, it played over 329 times and held the stage for nearly a century.[19] Its great popularity led Garrick to publish his acting edition in the same year of its original production, and it was reprinted steadily thereafter, on the average of once every three years until 1787.[20] Spranger Barry played Romeo and Mrs. Cibber (Theophilus Cibber's estranged second wife) played Juliet. Henry Woodward played Mercutio and Mrs. James the Nurse. When Barry left for Covent Garden in 1750, Garrick took over the role of Romeo and Miss Bellamy played Juliet. A rivalry between Garrick and Barry began, though both used basically the same acting version.[21]

As usual in eighteenth-century productions, Shakespeare's text was altered, although Garrick deserves credit (along with Cibber) for restoring a good deal of the original. The most notable alterations are the elimination of Lady Montague's role and Romeo's infatuation with Rosaline, as well as several changes in the last act. In the 1750 version, act 5 begins with an added scene—Juliet's funeral procession, complete with "dirges and much pomp."[22] Borrowing from Otway (as Cibber did, too), Garrick rewrote the final scene, interpolating some sixty-five lines of his own, so that Juliet awakens before Romeo dies. Somewhat deranged, Juliet at first does not recognize Romeo, who tries to get her to flee with him from the tomb. But it is too late. The poison begins to take effect just as Juliet realizes who is speaking to her. Romeo then takes an agonizing farewell from his beloved, bemoaning the "flinty hearts" of fathers so that "Children must be wretched." He dies in Juliet's arms, whose heart is also breaking at the sight.[23]

Garrick made many local alterations as well, shortening scenes and adding lines to bridge the cuts. The third act, for example, is half the length of the original, and Mercutio's pun on "grave man" is gone. Garrick curtailed Romeo's frantic ravings over being banished in 3.3; accordingly, Friar Lawrence's consoling speech is briefer. In 3.5, the scene moves from Juliet's bedroom to the garden, and her dialogue with her mother is shortened. In consequence, the ironic dialogue (ll. 80–103) disappears.[24] In keeping with his period's sense of decorum, Garrick eliminated much of the wordplay, especially the bawdry, as in the opening dialogue and in Mercutio's speeches. What later became known as "bowdlerization" continued until the present century, as many acting texts reveal.[25] On the other hand, as George Winchester Stone Jr. concludes, Garrick's version of *Romeo and Juliet* was "by far and away the best text of Shakespeare's play which carried on the stage from 1680 until 1846."[26]

The London theaters where *Romeo and Juliet* was performed—Drury Lane and Covent Garden—were large houses with proscenium stages that seated over a thousand spectators. A large platform stage stood before the proscenium arch and extended into the audience, some of whom actually sat on it or in stage boxes. The stage faced a raked pit where audiences did not stand, as in Shakespeare's Globe, but sat either there or in the surrounding galleries and boxes. Movable sets had been introduced since the time of the Restoration; these were invariably "stock" scenes, for example, "Church," "Court," "Towne," "Wood," after the scene locations Nicholas Rowe and Alexander Pope had inserted in their editions. Acting, as in Shakespeare's day, nevertheless continued mainly on the platform stage, only gradually receding in later years under the proscenium arch. Costumes were, again as before, contemporary dress: Barry and Garrick as Romeo wore knee-length coats over long waistcoats, knee breeches, and tie wigs (Barry even wore a three-cornered hat). Candles in chandeliers and footlights illuminated the stage until Garrick replaced them in the 1760s with candles mounted behind flats to focus on the actors' faces. Musical performances usually preceded serious drama, which was followed by an afterpiece or farce for a full evening's entertainment starting at 6:00 P.M.[27]

NINETEENTH-CENTURY PRODUCTIONS

By the middle of the nineteenth century, little had changed, except that—owing to uninspired revivals by John Philip Kemble and Edmund Kean, and the want of good actors for the male lead—*Romeo and Juliet* was less often performed. Garrick's text, slightly altered in Kemble's adaptation, continued to be used, despite other efforts to restore more of Shakespeare's texts on the London stage.[28] It remained for an American actress, Charlotte Cushman, to do for *Romeo and Juliet* what William Charles Macready (who incidentally had made his debut in London as Romeo in 1810) had done for *King Lear*. She restored much of the original text, as well as the order and structure of Shakespeare's scenes, and discarded the Garrick "flummery," such as the funeral procession and the ending. She herself assayed the role of Romeo and her sister Susan played Juliet—both very successfully.[29] It was not the first time Cushman had played Romeo; in the United States, she had enacted the part often between 1837 and 1845. Nor was she the first actress to undertake this "breeches" role. Ellen Tree had played Romeo in London, and fifteen other actresses had done so in America.[30]

Cushman's revival lasted eighty-four performances, beginning on December 29, 1845. Samuel Phelps followed her lead in his revival the next September, himself playing Mercutio, William Creswick and Laura Addison playing the lovers, and Mrs. H. Marston the Nurse: "a good cast, utterly lacking what Charlotte Cushman so richly supplied—the flash of genius."[31] Cushman's "genius" doubtless lay in her interpretation of Romeo, a role she reorganized so that his rise and fall, rather than that of both lovers, becomes the central focus of the tragedy. Although she may have thereby unbalanced the drama as a whole, she drew from it a Romeo who delighted nineteenth-century audiences: "the temperamental adolescent whose brief and extreme vicissitudes as a lover make him a pattern of tragic experience."[32]

Cushman's success, as Levenson says, broke Garrick's hold on Shakespeare's play and released it for a variety of productions for the next hundred years.[33] Not all of them succeeded, however, or succeeded totally. The famous Polish actress

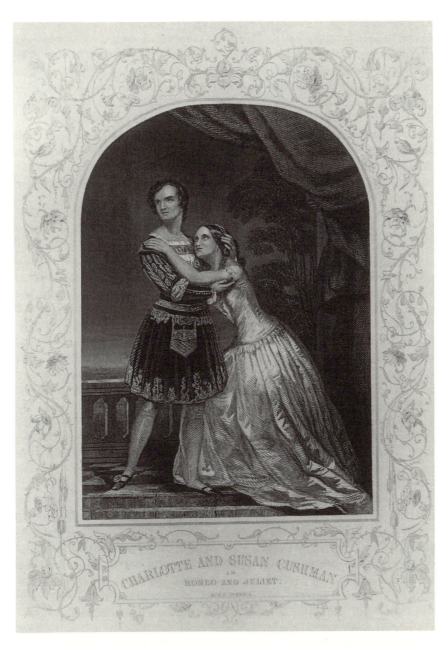

Charlotte and Susan Cushman as Romeo and Juliet. By permission of the Folger Shakespeare Library.

Helena Modjeska revived the play in 1881, playing Juliet to Johnston Forbes-Robertson's Romeo, but though sweet and sympathetic in the garden scene, she lacked force in the tragic ending.[34] Forbes-Robertson would rise to some acclaim later on as Romeo, but not until Henry Irving—at the age of forty-four!—decided to enact the role opposite Ellen Terry's Juliet in 1882. Not so much his age but his acting brought Irving criticism, such as this from William Winter: "Irving, distinctively and superlatively intellectual, overweighted the part of *Romeo*, seeming, while he conveyed all its meaning, to *expound* rather than to *impersonate* it."[35] William Teriss, who might better have exchanged roles with Irving, played Mercutio.[36] Irving's production was lavish, outdoing the elaborately pictorial productions for which the century became famous and which led to the reaction and innovations developed by William Poel, Gordon Craig, and Harley Granville-Barker at the end of the nineteenth and the beginning of the twentieth century.

The most famous Romeo of the nineteenth century was one of the last. In 1895, while Irving was on tour in America, Forbes-Robertson took over Irving's Lyceum Theatre for *Romeo and Juliet*. Trained by Samuel Phelps, Forbes-Robertson had not only the grace of movement and youth of person the role demands, but also "a sovereign beauty of voice and feature."[37] Thought and feeling were always in command in his performance. On Spranger Barry's gentlemanly lover he superimposed an overarching feeling of doom that above all identified the character.[38] Forbes-Robertson was the chief exponent of a newer style of acting, a more "naturalistic" or realistic kind of speaking, as against the more declamatory speech that hitherto had ruled the stage—doubtless occasioned, if not demanded, by huge theaters like the new Covent Garden, which could seat up to 3,000 spectators. Shakespeare's verse was spoken more like prose than poetry; action was toned down; "everything was to be refined and gentle."[39] Mrs. Patrick Campbell, who played Juliet, seems to have suffered from the same deficiencies as Ellen Terry in Irving's production, interesting and effective in the first half of the play, showing "something like girlish artlessness and grace" in the garden scene, but becoming "flaccid and ineffective" in the tragic passages.[40] The great comic actor Charles Coughlan was superb as Mercutio, a part well suited to his talents.

Meanwhile, from the middle of the eighteenth century onward, English companies toured America. The first of these companies was Lewis Hallam's, which began playing in Williamsburg, Virginia (1752–1753) and included *Romeo and Juliet* (Garrick's version) in its repertoire. Hallam's wife played Juliet, and after his death, Hallam's son Lewis Hallam Jr. played Romeo opposite his mother on at least one occasion.[41] Despite her increasingly matronly appearance, Mrs. Hallam (now Mrs. David Douglass) still retained both her beauty and her intelligence and was the principal actress of the company.[42]

Although American actors eventually supplanted, or at least rivaled, British imports by the next century, not until Charlotte Cushman brought her acclaimed London production to New York in 1850 did the first notable American *Romeo and Juliet* grace these shores.[43] The great American actor Edwin Booth mounted the play to inaugurate his newly erected theater in New York City in February 1869 and played Romeo opposite Mary McVicker's Juliet. Not the acting but the scenery attracted the greatest acclaim, for it was truly remarkable. McVicker was a poor choice as Juliet, lacking any of the graces that had come to be associated with the role, and Booth's Romeo was also seriously criticized, at least at first. Nevertheless, the production ran for ten weeks (fifty-eight performances) with "undiminished popularity."[44] A few years later, on November 27, 1875, California-born Mary Anderson, at the age of sixteen, made her debut as Juliet in Louisville, Kentucky, where she grew up. Then, after gaining experience in New York and elsewhere in America, she accepted an invitation in 1883 to occupy Irving's Lyceum Theatre in London. The following year, playing Juliet again, she mounted *Romeo and Juliet* in a splendidly scenic version that ran for a hundred nights. In 1885, Anderson brought her production, with Forbes-Robertson as Romeo, to America, where it received greater acclaim.[45]

Shakespeare's play gained popularity not only in the British Isles and in America, but also on the continent of Europe. In 1776, the French dramatist Jean-François Ducis (1733–1816) radically adapted *Romeo and Juliet*. He eliminated a host of parts, elevating the role of Montague to a major one for his friend, the actor Jean-Baptiste Brizard, who performed it.[46] In Germany, August Wilhelm Schlegel and Ludwig Tieck translated Shakespeare's play, but it was in Johann Wolfgang Goethe's radically revised version that *Romeo and Juliet* was performed in the early nineteenth century.[47] These productions and many others over the centuries throughout the Continent reflect changing tastes, as well as different cultures, to which Shakespeare's plays have been made to conform.

TWENTIETH-CENTURY PRODUCTIONS

By common consent, the landmark production of *Romeo and Juliet* in the early twentieth century was John Gielgud's at London's New Theatre (now the Albery) in 1935–1936.[48] Gielgud, who had begun his career as Romeo for Barry Jackson, again played Romeo, alternating with young Laurence Olivier as Mercutio. Peggy Ashcroft was Juliet, and Edith Evans played the Nurse.[49] Apart from the excellence of the acting, in which Gielgud and Olivier contrasted strongly in their performances as Romeo and in which Ashcroft was outstanding as Juliet, the major achievement of this production was the far fuller restoration of Shakespeare's text than the professional theater had seen for centuries. The script was based on the scholarly *Temple Shakespeare,* prepared from both Q1 and Q2, and included almost all of Shakespeare's bawdry, wit, and lyricism. Gielgud made a few minor cuts, however; the second Chorus was deleted, for example, as was the dialogue between Peter and the musicians in 4.5. Although the production was swiftly paced, performances ran to over three hours. So much for "this two hours' traffic of our stage"!

Gielgud's production is also noteworthy for its staging, fashioned by three young women known as the design team "Motley" (Percy and Sophia Harris and Elizabeth Montgomery). Elizabethan-style staging is what Gielgud, influenced by

Scene from Gielgud's 1935 production, with John Gielgud as Romeo and Peggy Ashcroft as Juliet. Motley designs. From the University of Illinois Motley Collection.

the experiments of Poel, Craig, and Granville-Barker, wanted, and Motley eagerly complied.[50] The basic stage set was a very simple one, placing the balcony center stage as a tower on columns, hollow underneath. Its inner spaces could be opened or closed by a curtain or shutters. Running diagonally across the stage was a set of black velvet curtains, which helped expedite scene changes. These were surmounted at the back by a strip of blue to suggest the hot Italian summer.[51] Costumes derived from Italian Renaissance paintings, especially those of Vittore Carpaccio, and tended to idealize the actors. Gielgud allowed only a single, twelve-minute interval after Mercutio's death. His intention, first and last, was to make the text work physically on the stage. He eschewed operatic arias, or "big moments," such as Juliet's potion-taking scene, and aimed for a fully integrated production in which even the smallest parts were carefully considered and performed. He succeeded admirably, setting box office records and establishing a new standard for *Romeo and Juliet* in the theater. His achievement is all the more remarkable insofar as he had only three weeks to prepare the production and rehearse the cast.

If Gielgud's production was a reaction against nineteenth-century excess, Peter Brook's in 1947 at Stratford-upon-Avon was in some ways a reaction against Gielgud. Brook had entirely opposite views regarding the text, or rather, he disregarded it as it suited him, cutting and otherwise modifying it to produce a script that he thought was more appropriate to the times. He defended his procedure, citing various earlier productions of *Romeo and Juliet* as "right" for their time just as, he felt, his was right for ours: "A production is only correct at the moment of its correctness, and only good at the moment of its success," he said.[52] In other words, he approached Shakespeare's play as living theater, not the "deadly theatre" that he described later in his book *The Empty Space*.

He chose young actors for his leads and was unconcerned that they could not "sing" their lines. He was more concerned with how the production looked—its visual images—than how it was spoken. Paul Scofield's Mercutio was perhaps the most memorable performance in that production. Rolf Gérard's basic set was unadorned—in fact, cold and austere—with little bits of isolated realism creating an effect that appeared "part fantasticated Giotto, part dream."[53] In Brook's view, *Romeo and Juliet* is "a play of youth, of freshness, of open air. . . . It is a play of wide spaces, in which all scenery and decoration easily become an irrelevance."[54] "Wide spaces," according to Levenson, is Brook's figurative expression for his sense of the text's psychological and emotional range, as well as his sense that the public scenes contributed vitally to the meaning and shape of the tragedy. Hence, he attempted to give modern theatrical expression to what he saw as a central theme in Shakespeare's text: "youth, energy, vitality crowded out of their living space by society, or the deadening customs and organization of an established community."[55] But despite Brook's eminent success with *Love's Labour's Lost* the previous season, his *Romeo and Juliet* was not critically acclaimed.[56] It remains more important to his own development as a director than to the stage history of the play.

The next important staging in Britain was Franco Zeffirelli's in 1960. Having made a success directing opera at Covent Garden, he was invited to mount *Romeo and Juliet* at the Old Vic. Meanwhile, in America, an adaptation of the play as a musical, *West Side Story* (1957), its music composed by Leonard Bernstein and its settings and characters updated to New York in the 1950s, became highly popular.[57] It was later made into a film—just as Zeffirelli later adapted his stage production into a film and watched it become, like *West Side Story,* immensely popular.

Zeffirelli's approach to his staging of *Romeo and Juliet* was even more radical than Brook's.[58] His aim was to make the play fully accessible to modern audiences, discarding the vestiges of romanticism that persisted despite Gielgud's and Brook's efforts and casting the leads with young, talented players who could perform naturally and realistically. His Verona was a real Italian city; his Montagues and Capulets real Italian families; his lovers deeply, passionately, youthfully in love. Like Brook, he was less interested, apparently, in the language than in visual effects; for Zeffirelli, poetry was conveyed as much by action as by words. "There is poetry," he said, ". . . in the Nurse bringing Juliet a bowl and a cloth for her toilet. This can call up a stream of ideas and facts connected with the daily life of Juliet and the Capulet household."[59]

John Stride played Romeo, Judi Dench played Juliet, and Alec McCowen was Mercutio. If critics complained that the characters failed to speak their lines "poetically" enough, they may have mistaken what the actors and Zeffirelli were attempting, which was, as John Russell Brown suggests, to render the poetry in a new and unfamiliar way.[60] This new way included changes of tempo, pitch, and volume—techniques Zeffirelli had developed while directing opera. "Shakespeare was writing to be *believed,*" Zeffirelli said, "so it is essential to make everything natural in every detail."[61] What he regarded as unbelievable or unnatural for a modern audience was cut. He simplified the diction and streamlined the action so that they became convincing to contemporary audiences. What impeded the fluency of action was discarded; thus, much of 4.5 was omitted. Altogether, he cut about a thousand lines, or a third of the full text, including Friar Lawrence's summation of events at the end of the play. In the latter instance, he may have erred, as Brown has remarked, echoing Granville-Barker's strictures, perhaps. The Friar's speech is important, even essential; replacing it with "a solemn, exotically illuminated dumb-show"—the bodies of Romeo and Juliet carried to the catafalque, the presumably reconciled families departing "with composed neatness" at opposite sides of the tomb, Benvolio and the Nurse reintroduced to take silent farewells of the bodies—all this seemed "empty and meaningless," even "pretentious and vague." It could hardly compensate for the Friar's speech, which underscores Shakespeare's theme at one of the play's most telling moments: how responsibility is learned through adversity.[62]

The production, despite some flaws, was nevertheless a success in large measure owing to the physical and emotional energy of the young lovers, although McCowen's rendition of Mercutio contributed as well. Zeffirelli invented a psychological history from a variety of nonhistorical sources for every scene.[63] Mercutio's Queen Mab speech became an integral part of his character development, not merely a set speech or aria. McCowen collapsed it into fragments of imagery, like a montage, and made it sound spontaneous—tense as well as witty. Mercutio no longer competed with Romeo as a romantic figure; when he died, the production did not become unbalanced, for it lost none of its romantic gusto or vigor. His duel with Tybalt, moreover, reflected a fresh, innovative approach: McCowen's Mercutio exhibited no skill as a duelist but responded to his opponent's threats as if they were a joke, just another opportunity to exhibit his bravura and entertain the youthful onlookers. The duel therefore became a kind of grotesque comedy, turning bitter purely by chance.[64]

The success of the world tour, in which Joanna Dunham replaced an exhausted Judi Dench, combined with huge profits from his film version of *The Taming of the Shrew,* starring Richard Burton and Elizabeth Taylor, may have led Zeffirelli to film *Romeo and Juliet* in 1968.[65] But given his cinematic approach to theater, it was only natural that he should go all the way now and make a film of what he had done, or tried to do, in his stage production. Again, he cast young actors for his leads. Though Olivia Hussey and Leonard Whiting were far less trained in Shakespeare than Dench and Stride, they looked their parts.[66] John McEnery was brilliant as Mercutio, playing him as deeply neurotic, his mental instability forcefully displayed as he delivered the Queen Mab speech.[67] Near the end of the century, Zeffirelli's film had become the most commercially successful Shakespeare film yet made.[68]

With all the advantages of film, Zeffirelli created a virtual Verona with a sprawling marketplace for the opening brawl, a palace for the ball scene, a Romanesque church for the wedding, and other equally impressive settings. He intensified Shakespeare's suggestions of violence in the first scene, shown here as extremely violent and bloody.[69] If he was criticized for a "rash, reckless style" by some, he nevertheless produced an overall highly effective and at times riveting film, "spectacular, extravagant, full of nervous motion, energy, camera movement, rapid cutting."[70] He was no mere popularizer of Shakespeare but someone who had thought deeply about the play he was filming while remaining mindful of the mass audience that awaited his efforts. The result was a colorful, beautifully designed, musically enhanced film that, as Jack Jorgens remarks, revealed fresh interpretative truths about the play as well. For example, in Zeffirelli's view, Lady Capulet is the "hub" of the continuing feud between the families; she has a less than happy marriage, is attracted to the young, virile Tybalt, and experiences a nascent jealousy of her daughter.[71]

Once again, Zeffirelli stood accused of sacrificing good verse speaking for other effects, and he cut the text by about two thirds. Of course, as in other Shakespeare films, the camera compensates, translating visual for verbal imagery, although at times in this one, the camera and the text were at odds, for example, when Romeo describes Juliet at the ball as "a snowy dove trooping with crows." Attractive as Hussey might be, she was hardly a "snowy dove," and the splendid ladies dancing with her were anything but "crows."[72] Nevertheless, Zeffirelli successfully released many aspects latent in Shakespeare's text, especially those that appealed to the young, such as pacifism, distrust of elders, and sexual liberation.[73]

One of the most memorable aspects of Zeffirelli's film is the musical score by Nino Rota, which, according to Albert Cirillo, provided "sonic coloring, and punctuation . . . to the color photography itself."[74] The neo-Elizabethan ballad "What Is a Youth?" written by Eugene Walter and vocalized by Glenn Weston became popular in its own right; but in the film it reflected the two-part design, or the division into light and love in the first part, and darkness and death in the second, the two parts separated by an intermission after the wedding.[75] Rota's music was anything but Elizabethan, but it was made to sound so, even as modern instrumentation replaced the "broken consort" of the Elizabethan playhouse. Similarly, Alberto Testa's choreography in the ball scene not only emphasized the gap between generations (a major social problem of the late sixties), but also adapted Elizabethan dances to modern taste while Romeo and Juliet, on the fringes peering in, emblematized the isolation of young lovers from adult life.[76] By every account a "youth movie," a Renaissance equivalent of *The Graduate,* as Jorgens says (*Shakespeare on Film,* p. 86), it became a standard representation of the play for school use—far better in many respects than the "museum Shakespeare" that the British Broadcasting Corporation's production offered in its first series of Shakespeare plays on videotape in 1979.

More recently, a literal updating of *Romeo and Juliet,* both on the stage and on the screen, has become increasingly evident. In the Royal Shakespeare Company's production in 1986, directed by Michael Bogdanov, present-day Verona was the setting, designed by Chris Dyer. Dubbed the "Alfa-Romeo and Juliet" by a waggish critic, because in 3.1 Tybalt (played by Hugh Quarshie) drove on stage in a sports car, the production even incorporated a swimming pool around which bored Veronese youth sat recovering from their previous night's debauch, dropping Alka-Seltzer into their drinks. Against this modern backdrop, the characters were played as contemporary types: teenage gang members, Italian business tycoons, socially ambitious wives, all contributing great vitality to performances.[77]

In any transposing of time frames, certain adjustments become necessary. Props need to be modified—switchblade knives for rapiers, for example—and dialogue occasionally must be altered. Thus in Bogdanov's production, the Capulets' ball became a swinging party complete with rock music, and Romeo killed himself with a hypodermic needle filled with drugs. But the production never became *West Side Story* in blank verse. Sean Bean was a more than credible Romeo who served Niamh Cusack's Juliet, in her own words, "one hundred per cent in the vulnerability and total commitment of his playing a young boy in love."[78] Cusack herself was an excellent Juliet, alienated from her domineering mother but exuding a joyous disposition, notwithstanding the nouveau riche aspirations of her family and even the Nurse, played by Dilys Laye. Although the Nurse failed as a confidante, this interpretation explained Juliet's early loneliness and later self-reliance.[79]

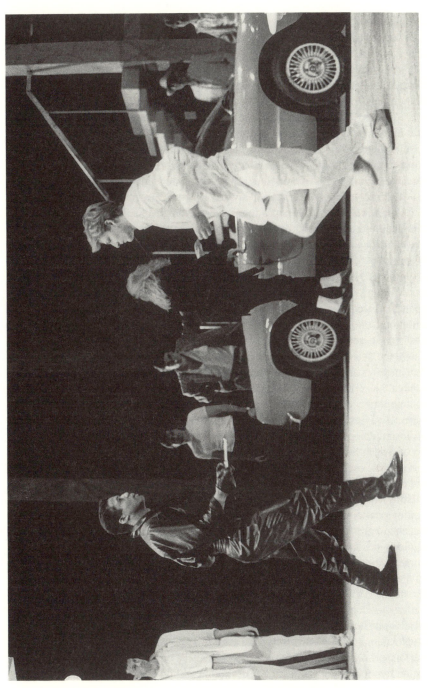

The "Alfa Romeo and Juliet" (1986) with Hugh Quarshie as Tybalt and Sean Bean as Romeo. Joe Cocks Studio Collection, Shakespeare Centre Library.

Bogdanov cut and shaped the playscript to emphasize the decadence of this corrupt society and bring into greater relief the innocent love of Romeo and Juliet, which in that environment stood no chance for complete fulfillment. The last scene was divided in two. After discovering Romeo's body, Juliet swiftly impaled herself on a knife she had placed in his hands, thus drawing attention to the proximity of death and love that is one of the play's important subtexts.[80] A brief blackout followed, used to prepare for a media event, complete with paparazzi, camcorders, and television personnel. Gilded statues of the dead lovers were then unveiled, but in this context they did less to honor Romeo and Juliet than to drive home the point about their lives gone to waste in a society controlled by materialist values. The Chorus, which Shakespeare had intended as a Prologue, was finally heard, altered to the past tense and spoken by the Prince.[81]

Bogdanov's modern-dress production directly or indirectly influenced two other productions and doubtless many more. On November 18, 1997, the Source Theater Company began its run at the Folger Library's Elizabethan Theatre. Romeo and his friends were young parochial schoolboys, dressed in blue blazers, khaki trousers, and red and blue rep ties. Juliet's girlfriends (added to the dramatis personae) also wore school uniforms, when they were not sporting blue jeans, black lace-up boots, and sleeveless tops. Once again, the Montagues and Capulets were socially ambitious, middle-class, middle-aged couples, and Juliet's Nurse a well-coifed and well-manicured servant who looked rather odd in a housemaid's uniform. Friar Lawrence became Father Lawrence, the local parish priest doing his best to educate his boys in good Catholic doctrine. Joe Banno, the director, explained the design of his production as Peter Brook had defended his: if Shakespeare used contemporary dress, why not reimagine *Romeo and Juliet* for today? "What if these teenagers were suburban Everykids," he said in a program note, "haunting malls and raves and channel-surfing their young lives away in Verona (*read*: Fairfax or South Jersey or whatever works for you)?" The boys carried switchblades and pistols, rock music played loudly from the moment one entered the theater, and instead of a ball, the Capulets were hosts to—what else?—a barbecue.

Holly Twyford as Juliet and John Worley as Romeo easily conveyed the impression of young teenagers in love. Sporting an earring, a crew cut, and obviously bleached hair, Benvolio, played by Christopher Borg, was anything but the quiet, studious young man of Shakespeare's conception. Mercutio (Paul Takacs) was worse, a loud and disrespectful boor. The duel between him and Tybalt (Johnny Ray Meeks) took place, not in a marketplace or the parking lot of a mall (the Folger stage is, after all, quite small), but in Father Lawrence's classroom. Switchblades were used, but Romeo unaccountably turned coward after dueling with Tybalt and shot him with a pistol several times. Juliet received the bad news from the Nurse, not in her room, but in the schoolroom, where she found the Nurse, disconsolate, holding a bloody piece of cloth. At the end, after Romeo killed himself with a hypodermic syringe and Juliet followed him the same way, everyone appeared on stage, including Benvolio and the Nurse, to mourn the lovers. Although Banno cut much of the text (e.g., all of 5.2), he retained Friar Lawrence's explana-

The Folger Shakespeare Theater production (1997), with Holly Twyford as Juliet, Megan Morgan as Lady Capulet, and Cam Magee as the Nurse. K. W. Cobb for the Folger Shakespeare Library.

tion of events, thus preserving to some extent Shakespeare's complex emotional conclusion.

The evening I saw the production (the last night of previews), the audience was composed largely of schoolchildren, teenagers who seemed to like the performance almost as much as they must have liked Baz Luhrmann's 1996 film version, set in Verona Beach, south Florida. This is a film clearly intended for young people, the MTV generation. Like the updated stage productions, it has all the trappings of decadent contemporary society: images of sexual promiscuity, alcohol and substance abuse, urban decay, civil unrest, guns of every type, and a private code of personal violence masquerading as honor.[82] Perhaps borrowing from Bogdanov's ending, Luhrmann used a TV anchorwoman to frame the tragedy as a feature news story. Father Lawrence, expertly played by Peter Postlethwaite, fantasizes about using Romeo and Juliet's marriage to end the feud, a fantasy rendered visible on screen. As in Zeffirelli's film, the text is heavily cut, and for the same reasons. The camera provides the images Shakespeare used his verse to convey, however different those images now appear (e.g., lots of crosses, rotary candles, and other Catholic emblems). Contrasting with the metropolis of Verona Beach, Mantua is a wasteland of dirt roads and trailer homes. There Romeo finds the Apothecary in a poolroom, where he lives. Of course.

The Capulets and Montagues here are not so much middle-class as competing Mafia families, although the Capulets appear more like Mediterranean types and the Montagues northern European. Mercutio (Harold Perrineau) and the Prince (now Captain Prince, Verona's chief of police), both played by African Americans, add further racial overtones. Though by no means effeminate, Mercutio wears drag to the ball and is highly protective—even possessive—of Romeo. He intimates that Queen Mab is a drug and slips Romeo something, possibly LSD, to convince him to come to the ball. Drugs and alcohol pervade the scene; Capulet attacks his disobedient daughter while obviously drunk and must be restrained by his wife and the Nurse. Even Father Lawrence drinks heavily and needs to be helped before saying mass. At the ball—more a rock music disco than a cotillion—Juliet (Claire Danes) appears in a white gown with wings on her back; Romeo (Leonardo DiCaprio) dresses in a suit of shining armor. Immediately attracted to each other, they frolic in the Capulets' swimming pool in the garden scene, having played a game of hide-and-seek with others earlier at the ball.

Two scenes convey the essence of the film and its interpretation of Shakespeare's play. In 3.1, Tybalt stands ready to fight a duel with Romeo as an affair of honor, and his friends prepare him accordingly. Mercutio likewise attempts to prepare Romeo, who stops him and walks slowly toward Tybalt to talk him out of fighting. When Romeo refuses to fight, Tybalt beats him savagely, kicking him on the ground mercilessly until Mercutio intervenes and challenges him instead. They do not use guns but brawl with clubs and broken glass from an abandoned theater where the fight has moved. Tybalt stabs Mercutio with a piece of this glass, then flees in his car. Romeo chases him, yelling madly, until Tybalt's car overturns and the two grapple for a gun, with which Romeo almost seems to want to commit sui-

The Folger Shakespeare Theater production (1977), with Paul Takacs as Mercutio, John Worley as Romeo, and Johnny Ray Meeks as Tybalt. K. W. Cobb for the Folger Shakespeare Library.

cide as much as to kill Tybalt. Startled by Romeo's suicidal fury, Tybalt backs away; Romeo shoots him and is left utterly drained and wasted. Together with the death of Mercutio, the incident suggests to the audience, as Robert Kole says, that there is no glory in hatred, no honor in violence.

The last scene is likewise reshaped to fit Luhrmann's conception. Juliet's body rests in the church, lit by hundreds of candles like a shrine, when Romeo enters. No Paris intrudes, nor does Father Lawrence come to save Juliet when she awakens. The lovers are isolated in death, as they were in life. Just as Romeo drinks the poison, Juliet stirs; and on the verge of death, Romeo sees that Juliet is alive. They kiss as he dies. Juliet takes his gun and, with it, kills herself. They have been tricked by fate, as much victims of a world beyond their control as headstrong teenagers governed by strong passions and impulsive acts. An ambulance arrives to carry the bodies away, but there are no speeches, no gestures of reconciliation, no end, apparently, to the feud. Nothing has changed.

Whether in Elizabethan costume or in modern dress, heavily cut or textually complete, *Romeo and Juliet* continues to rank with *Hamlet* as among the most frequently performed of Shakespeare's tragedies. Recent film adaptations have only contributed to the play's popularity and its appeal to young audiences. It may be adapted to carry a social or other ideological message, as Michael Kahn's Folger production did in 1986. He staged the play partly to warn against the dangers of teenage suicide, which was then rising to near-epidemic proportions in the United States.[83] Productions may emphasize the star-crossed lovers motif announced in the Prologue, or they may show the young lovers culpably bringing disaster upon themselves by their impulsiveness. Or they may stress the hopelessness of a young and innocent love in a world governed by power struggles, violence, and greed. As the play's performance history shows, its appeal is perennial, and not only in the form Shakespeare has given us. The play has inspired over two dozen operas and ballets by such notables as Hector Berlioz, Pyotr Ilich Tchaikovsky, Charles-François Gounod, Sergey Sergeyevich Prokofiev, and others. No wonder. The story was popular long before Shakespeare, who has given it consummate expression, and it will continue to remain popular as long as young people still find poetry and each other irresistible.

NOTES

1. The company later became famous as the King's Men when it fell under the patronage of James I in 1603. For a brief period in 1596–1597, before George succeeded his father as the Lord Chamberlain, it was known as the Lord Hunsdon's Men, since the Careys were the Lords Hunsdon. See E. K. Chambers, *The Elizabethan Stage*, 4 vols. (Oxford: Clarendon Press, 1923), vol. 2, pp. 193–95, and Andrew Gurr, *The Shakespearian Playing Companies* (Oxford: Clarendon Press, 1996), p. 279.

2. See T. W. Baldwin, *The Organization and Personnel of the Shakespearean Company* (Princeton, N.J.: Princeton University Press, 1927), pp. 268–69. Baldwin, however, dates the play to an earlier period, 1590–1591, than most scholars now accept.

3. T. J. King, *Casting of Shakespeare's Plays: London Actors and Their Roles, 1590–1642* (Cambridge: Cambridge University Press, 1992), pp. 82–83 and tables 42 and 43. On doubling of parts, see Giorgio Melchiori, "Peter, Balthasar, and Shakespeare's Art of Doubling," *Modern Language Review* 78 (1983): 777–92.

4. Chambers, *Elizabethan Stage*, vol. 2, pp. 402–3. In "The Date and Expected Venue of *Romeo and Juliet*," *Shakespeare Survey* 49 (1996): 19, Andrew Gurr says that Shakespeare most likely had Burbage's Theatre in mind when he wrote this play.

5. The reconstructed Globe on London's Southbank, opened for regular performances in the summer of 1997, revealed this difference in audience experience between those who sat in the galleries and those who stood around the stage.

6. Chambers, *Elizabethan Stage*, vol. 2, p. 403.

7. Note that these costumes reflected contemporary taste in dress. Historically motivated designs did not enter stage production until the nineteenth century.

8. See Gibbons's note to the stage directions in his New Arden edition (London: Methuen, 1980). He says that the transition now makes the main stage Juliet's bedroom, whereas it had just been located "aloft." Elizabethan audiences apparently had no problem with such transitions, but I do not see why the space must still be Juliet's bedroom and not some other room in the Capulet house.

9. Evans, ed., *New Cambridge Shakespeare* (Cambridge: Cambridge University Press, 1984), p. 33. In *Elizabethan Stage Conditions* (Cambridge: Cambridge University Press, 1931), p. 40, M. C. Bradbrook maintains that even Elizabethan credulity would be strained to see Romeo attack the traverse with a mattock and spade. Cp. Graham Holderness, *William Shakespeare: "Romeo and Juliet,"* Penguin Critical Studies (London: Penguin Books, 1990), pp. 59–65. Following G. W. Williams's note in his old-spelling critical edition (Durham, N.C.: Duke University Press, 1964), p. 147, Holderness rejects the concept of an inner stage and argues that Juliet remained on her bed from 4.3 to 5.3, hidden by the bed's own curtains during most of the action after the Nurse discovers her in 4.5. Neither he nor Williams indicates how Tybalt's body is also found in 5.3.

10. This is the scenario C. Walter Hodges suggests. See his drawings in Evans's edition, p. 32. Cp. Leslie Thomson, " 'With patient ears attend': *Romeo and Juliet* on the Elizabethan Stage," *Studies in Philology* 92 (1995): 230–47, esp. pp. 241–43. Thomson suggests that Romeo's language as much as (or more than) anything else helped the audience visualize the action; that the bed in 4.5 probably remained on stage until 5.3; and that the transition from bed to bier was thematically justified and intentional. See also Alan C. Dessen's chapter, " 'Romeo opens the tomb,' " in *Recovering Shakespeare's Theatrical Vocabulary* (Cambridge: Cambridge University Press, 1995), pp. 176–95, esp. pp. 190–95. Using Richard Hosley's distinction between "theatrical" and "fictional" stage directions—that is, those that are directed at an actor versus those that merely "tell a story"—Dessen discusses various ways of staging 5.3. He favors a "minimalist" approach rather than a more literalistic one in which a tomb property is brought on stage. He suggests (p. 190) that Tybalt's body may not actually have been displayed but is only conjured up in the audience's imagination by Romeo's words (ll. 97–100). Similarly, if the Q1 stage directions (implicit in the Q2 dialogue) are understood as fictional rather than theatrical, Paris strews his flowers and sweet water, not on or around a verisimilar structure, but on some unlocalized space that his words then help to define. Romeo's action in opening the tomb may likewise be performed in minimalist fashion. For further discussion of the tomb scene, see Gurr, "Date and Expected Venue," pp. 22–25. Gurr favors use of the trapdoor as the tomb.

11. Jill Levenson, *Shakespeare in Performance: "Romeo and Juliet"* (Manchester: Manchester University Press, 1987), p. 15.

12. *The London Stage, 1660–1800,* ed. William Van Lennep (Carbondale: Southern Illinois University Press, 1965), part 1, pp. 22, 48.

13. Quoted in Evans, ed., *New Cambridge Shakespeare,* p. 33, and Katherine L. Wright, *Shakespeare's "Romeo and Juliet" in Performance: Traditions and Departures* (Lewiston, N.Y.: Edwin Mellen Press, 1997), p. 50. Wright also cites Hazelton Spencer's explanation that Pepys was in a bad mood that day, beset with worries about his financial situation and having quarreled with others before coming to the theater. He could be a severe critic, as his comments on the revival of *A Midsummer Night's Dream* also reveal.

14. *Roscius Anglicanus* (London, 1708); cited by Stanley Wells, "The Challenges of *Romeo and Juliet,*" *Shakespeare Survey* 49 (1996): 2.

15. Hazelton Spencer, *Shakespeare Improved* (Cambridge, Mass.: Harvard University Press, 1927), p. 292.

16. See Charles Beecher Hogan, *Shakespeare in the Theatre, 1701–1800,* 2 vols. (Oxford: Clarendon Press, 1952), vol. 1, pp. 404–10. Besides a brief summary of the scenes, Hogan provides cast lists for many performances.

17. Quoted in Spencer, *Shakespeare Improved,* p. 297.

18. Levenson, *Shakespeare in Performance,* pp. 18–19.

19. George Winchester Stone Jr., "*Romeo and Juliet*: The Source of Its Modern Stage Career," in *Shakespeare 400,* ed. James G. McManaway (New York: Holt, Rinehart, and Winston, 1964), pp. 191–92.

20. Ibid., p. 195.

21. Hogan, *Shakespeare in the Theatre,* vol. 1, pp. 411–12; Stone, "Source," pp. 192, 195. For the competition that arose between Garrick and Barry, who played Romeo in different theaters, see Stone, ibid., pp. 195–97. To heighten the spectacle, Garrick later added a "Masquerade Dance" in act 1 and Juliet's funeral procession at the start of act 5, both of which became very popular in productions.

22. George C. D. Odell, *Shakespeare from Betterton to Irving,* 2 vols. (New York: Scribner's, 1920), vol. 1, p. 345; Hogan, *Shakespeare in the Theatre,* vol. 1, p. 405. Stone reprints Garrick's words to the dirge in "Source," p. 203, the music for which was discovered and published by Charles Haywood in *Shakespeare Quarterly* 11 (1960): 173–88.

23. Odell, *Betterton to Irving,* vol. 1, pp. 345–47, reprints part of this last scene and quotes Francis Gentleman's approving words in 1770, which claimed that "no play ever received greater advantage from alteration. . . . [B]ringing Juliet to life before Romeo dies, is undoubtedly a change of infinite merit." Stone, "Source," pp. 199–206, likewise reprints Garrick's revision of the ending and discusses other changes, for instance, the deletion of the Prologue, the rearrangement of scenes in act 1, the alteration of certain rhymes, and the omission of puns, especially bawdy ones. Juliet's age is also changed—to eighteen. The emendations were, as Stone says, typical of mid-eighteenth-century decorum and rationalism.

24. Stone, "Source," p. 202.

25. See, for example, Kemble's promptbook of 1811, which was based on Garrick's edition and is reproduced in facsimile in *John Philip Kemble Promptbooks,* ed. Charles Shattuck (Charlottesville: University Press of Virginia for Folger Shakespeare Library, 1974), vol. 8, pp. 1–75. In some American schools, bowdlerized texts are still used in classes for children in the ninth and tenth grades.

26. Stone, "Source," p. 206. For another detailed analysis of Garrick's version, see Levenson, *Shakespeare in Performance,* pp. 19–30.

27. Levenson, *Shakespeare in Performance*, pp. 26–27; Evans, ed., *New Cambridge Shakespeare*, pp. 41–43. Evans, p. 37, reproduces a playbill for Garrick's production of *Romeo and Juliet* at Drury Lane on November 16, 1756, which highlights not only the names of the principal actors, but also the "Funeral Procession to the Monument of the Capulets" and the French farce, *The Anatomist*, performed at the end of the evening. For further discussion of the ways that eighteenth-century theaters affected staging, see Donald C. Mullin, "Theatre Structure and Its Effect on Production," in *The Stage and the Page*, ed. George Winchester Stone Jr. (Berkeley: University of California Press, 1981), pp. 73–89.

28. Nicola Vaccai's, Vincenzo Bellini's, and Charles-François Gounod's operas all followed the Garrick text as late as 1867. In these operas, Juliet awakens before Romeo dies, and the lovers sing a last duet (Wright, *Performance*, p. 133).

29. See William Winter, *Shakespeare on the Stage*, 2nd series (New York: Moffat, Yard, 1915), pp. 205–11, and Charles Shattuck, *Shakespeare on the American Stage*, 2 vols. (Washington, D.C.: Folger Library, 1976–1987), vol. 1, pp. 92–94. Winter and Shattuck cite several contemporary accounts of Cushman's production and its revivals.

30. Levenson, *Shakespeare in Performance*, p. 32; Odell, *Betterton to Irving*, vol. 2, pp. 271–72.

31. Odell, *Betterton to Irving*, vol. 2, p. 272. Cp. Wright, *Performance*, pp. 134–38.

32. Levenson, *Shakespeare in Performance*, p. 35.

33. Ibid., p. 40.

34. Odell, *Betterton to Irving*, vol. 2, p. 377.

35. Winter, *Shakespeare on the Stage*, p. 132.

36. Odell, *Betterton to Irving*, vol. 2, p. 378.

37. Robert Speaight, *Shakespeare on the Stage* (London: Collins, 1973), p. 122.

38. Wright, *Performance*, p. 141. Cp. Winter, *Shakespeare on the Stage*, p. 136, on his portrayal as "intense, fervidly emotional, profoundly sincere, subtly suffused with an elusive spiritual quality ominous of predestinate ruin, artistically finished in every detail of action, and conveyed through the medium of a clear, refined, exquisite elocution, delicious to hear." After playing Romeo in Modjeska's production, Forbes-Robertson had performed in America in 1885 with Mary Anderson. What he lost in youth, Odell says (*Betterton to Irving*, vol. 2, p. 389), he gained in "authority and poetic fervour" ten years later.

39. Odell, *Betterton to Irving*, vol. 2, pp. 414–15.

40. Winter, *Shakespeare on the Stage*, p. 137.

41. Shattuck, *American Stage*, vol. 1, p. 11, refers to this "odd little Oedipean situation, which may have aroused wonder in the more knowing observers but was no cause for the gouging out of eyes." Winter, *Shakespeare on the Stage*, p. 157, notes that Fanny Kemble acted Juliet on October 1, 1832, in New York opposite a Romeo played by her father, Charles Kemble. Later, Charlotte and Susan Cushman, sisters, played opposite each other, disturbing Edinburgh audiences but not those in London (Shattuck, *American Stage*, vol. 1, pp. 92–93).

42. Shattuck, *American Stage*, vol. 1, pp. 9–11.

43. George C. D. Odell, *Annals of the New York Stage*, 15 vols. (New York: Columbia University Press, 1927–1949), vol. 5, p. 575.

44. Shattuck, *American Stage*, vol. 1, pp. 135–40. Like Cushman's, Booth's production was based on Shakespeare's original text, but heavily cut, partly because of the need for scene shifting. Dissatisfied with his Romeo, Booth never essayed the role again. Cp. Winter, *Shakespeare on the Stage*, pp. 161–65.

45. Shattuck, *American Stage*, vol. 2, pp. 103–7; Winter, *Shakespeare on the Stage*, pp. 172–79. Winter claimed to have seen Anderson play Juliet about thirty-five times and re-

garded her performance as superior to those of Adelaide Neilson, Helena Modjeska, Ellen Terry, or any other actress he had seen in the role (p. 177).

46. Speaight, *Shakespeare on the Stage,* p. 89.

47. Ibid., pp. 105–6.

48. See, for example, Levenson, *Shakespeare in Performance,* pp. 46–63, from which many of the details in this section are drawn, and Wright, *Performance,* pp. 195–249.

49. For analyses of these performances, besides Levenson's and Wright's, see J. C. Trewin, *Shakespeare on the English Stage, 1900–1964* (London: Barrie and Rockliff, 1964), pp. 152–53, and James Agate, *Brief Chronicles* (London: Cape, 1943), pp. 208–15. Despite criticism of his verse speaking, Agate said of Olivier that he was "the most moving Romeo I have ever seen" (p. 210).

50. See Michael Mullin's *Design by Motley* (Newark: University of Delaware Press, 1995), pp. 47–51. Mullin and Levenson reproduce photographs, drawings, and diagrams. See also Speaight, *Shakespeare on the Stage,* pp. 146, 154.

51. Mullin, *Motley,* p. 48.

52. Quoted from Brook's essay, "Style in Shakespearean Production," by Levenson, *Shakespeare in Performance,* p. 81. The essay appears in *Orpheus* 1 (1948), reprinted in *The Modern Theatre,* ed. Daniel Selzer (Boston: Little, Brown, 1967).

53. Cited from contemporary reviews by Levenson, *Shakespeare in Performance,* p. 71; for illustrations of stage sets, see p. 44.

54. Cited from Brook's "Style in Shakespearean Production," ibid., p. 73.

55. Ibid., p. 72.

56. See Trewin, *Shakespeare on the English Stage,* pp. 205–6.

57. See Robert Hapgood, "*West Side Story* and the Modern Appeal of *Romeo and Juliet,*" *Shakespeare Jahrbuch* 8 (1972): 99–112; reprinted in *"Romeo and Juliet": Critical Essays,* ed. John F. Andrews (New York: Garland, 1993), pp. 229–41. For *West Side Story,* Stephen Sondheim composed the lyrics, Arthur Laurents wrote the book, and Jerome Robbins choreographed. Hapgood shows how a modern adaptation can be a form of critical interpretation of the original, "its emphases and omissions, successes and failures serving to sharpen our awareness of the original and its modern appeal." The film version (1961) won ten Academy Awards.

58. See Levenson, *Shakespeare in Performance,* pp. 84–104. Many of the following comments derive from her description and analysis. Cp. Peter Holding, *"Romeo and Juliet": Text and Performance* (London: Macmillan, 1992), pp. 45–51.

59. Cited by Levenson, *Shakespeare in Performance,* p. 89.

60. John Russell Brown, "S. Franco Zeffirelli's *Romeo and Juliet,*" *Shakespeare Survey* 15 (1962): 149. The essay is reprinted in John Russell Brown, *Shakespeare's Plays in Performance* (London: Edward Arnold, 1966), pp. 167–79, and includes photographs of the production. Brown gives several examples of this new way of presenting the verse. For a contrary view, see Speaight, *Shakespeare on the Stage,* pp. 272–73.

61. Cited by Levenson, *Shakespeare in Performance,* p. 90.

62. Brown, "Zeffirelli's *Romeo and Juliet,*" pp. 152–53. Cp. Holding, *Text and Performance,* pp. 50–51, who makes a similar point.

63. Levenson, *Shakespeare in Performance,* p. 93, gives several examples: for instance, Friar Lawrence's background before he became a priest and Romeo's early pretense of being in love so that people would notice him.

64. Holding, *Text and Performance,* p. 49. Zeffirelli directed the scene much the same way in his film version. See his explanation in *Staging Shakespeare,* ed. Glenn Loney (New

York: Garland, 1990), p. 251. He wanted the duel not only to reflect Mercutio's personality, but to contrast with the second duel, between Tybalt and Romeo, which he felt has to be much more serious and intense.

65. Levenson, *Shakespeare in Performance,* p. 104.

66. In fact, Hussey and Whiting were younger than Dench and Stride, but Zeffirelli insisted on actors who were "the right age," that is, as close to fourteen and a little older as possible. See *Staging Shakespeare,* ed. Loney, pp. 257–58.

67. For an acute analysis of this scene and the misogynist content of Mercutio's speech, see Peter S. Donaldson, *Shakespearean Films/Shakespearean Directors* (Boston: Unwin Hyman, 1990), pp. 158–59. Donaldson, like Joseph Porter, sees the interplay of hetero- and homosexual eros as central, but Zeffirelli's Mercutio in the film is more confused and troubled than Porter seems to think: "Zeffirelli reads Mercutio's mix of desire and contempt for male intimacy not as evidence of cultural heterogeneity but as dissonances and confusions within an individual psyche struggling with the issue of sexual identity" (p. 186 n. 26).

68. Ibid., p. 145.

69. Jay L. Halio, "Zeffirelli's *Romeo and Juliet*: The Camera versus the Text," *Literature/Film Quarterly* 5 (1977): 322–23.

70. Jack J. Jorgens, *Shakespeare on Film* (Bloomington: Indiana University Press, 1977), pp. 80–81.

71. Ibid., pp. 83–84.

72. Halio, "Camera versus Text," p. 323.

73. Donaldson, *Shakespearean Films,* p. 145. In his chapter " 'Let Lips Do What Hands Do': Male Bonding, Eros, and Loss in Zeffirelli's *Romeo and Juliet,*" pp. 145–88, Donaldson also argues that Zeffirelli brought to the surface the homoerotic aspects of Shakespeare's art.

74. Cited by Kenneth Rothwell, "Zeffirelli's *Romeo and Juliet*: Words into Picture and Music," *Literature/Film Quarterly* 5 (1977): 327, from Albert Cirillo, "The Art of Franco Zeffirelli and Shakespeare's *Romeo and Juliet,*" *Tri-Quarterly* 16 (1969): 68–93.

75. Rothwell, ibid., p. 327. Rothwell refers to the "bloom" of youth in the opening lines and the "fading" in the last lines.

76. Ibid., pp. 328–29.

77. Holding, *Text and Performance,* p. 63. Although I saw this production in Stratford-upon-Avon in 1986, Holding's account has been a useful reminder of many of its details.

78. *Players of Shakespeare 2,* ed. Russell Jackson and Robert Smallwood (Cambridge: Cambridge University Press, 1988), pp. 122–23; cited by Holding, ibid., p. 64.

79. Holding, ibid., p. 65.

80. Ibid., p. 67.

81. Jay L. Halio, *Understanding Shakespeare's Plays in Performance* (Manchester: Manchester University Press, 1988), p. 78, and Holding, ibid., p. 67.

82. See Robert Kole's review and Peter Newman's article, "Luhrmann's Young Lovers as Seen by Their Peers," both in *Shakespeare Bulletin* 15 (1997): 33–35 and 36–37, respectively, from which I have drawn some details and comments. For a comparison of Lurhmann's film with Trevor Nunn's *Twelfth Night,* see Stanley Kauffmann, "Blanking Verse," *The New Republic,* December 2, 1996, pp. 40, 42.

83. See Halio, *Understanding,* pp. 78–79.

SELECTED BIBLIOGRAPHY

EDITIONS

Evans, G. B., ed. *Romeo and Juliet.* In *New Cambridge Shakespeare.* Cambridge: Cambridge University Press, 1984. Based on the second quarto (1599), with passages from Q1 in the collation. Fully annotated with extensive introduction.

Gibbons, Brian, ed. *Romeo and Juliet.* New Arden edition. London: Methuen, 1980. Based on Q2. Fully annotated with collations and extensive introduction. Substantial extracts from Arthur Brooke's *Romeus and Juliet* in an appendix.

Levenson, Jill, ed. *Romeo and Juliet.* Oxford: Oxford University Press (forthcoming). Based on Q2. Fully annotated with collations and extensive introduction. Includes a modern-spelling edition of Q1 in an appendix.

Williams, George Walton, ed. *Romeo and Juliet.* Durham, NC: Duke University Press, 1964. An original-spelling edition based on Q2 with textual introduction; extensive bibliographical, staging, and textual notes; and collations.

TEXTUAL STUDIES

Farley-Hills, David. "The 'Bad' Quarto of *Romeo and Juliet.*" *Shakespeare Survey* 49 (1996): 27–44. Q1 is not a memorial reconstruction, but a stage abridgment by someone other than Shakespeare.

Foster, Donald W. "The Webbing of *Romeo and Juliet.*" In *Critical Essays on "Romeo and Juliet,"* ed. Joseph A. Porter. New York: G. K. Hall, 1997, pp. 131–49. Q1 preceded Q2 in composition; Shakespeare revised and expanded the version from which Q1 derives.

Greg, W. W. *The Shakespeare First Folio.* Oxford: Clarendon Press, 1955. A textual and bibliographical analysis of all the plays in the First Folio.

Halio, Jay L. "Handy-Dandy: Q1/Q2 *Romeo and Juliet.*" In *Shakespeare's "Romeo and Juliet": Texts, Contexts, and Interpretation,* ed. Jay L. Halio. Newark: University of Delaware Press, 1995, pp. 123–50. Q1 is basically Shakespeare's abridgment of the Q2 version for the stage.

Hoppe, Harry. *The Bad Quarto of "Romeo and Juliet."* Ithaca, N.Y.: Cornell University Press, 1948. A thorough analysis of Q1 as a memorial reconstruction by the actors who played Romeo and Paris.

Ioppolo, Grace. *Revising Shakespeare.* Cambridge, Mass.: Harvard University Press, 1991. A study of Shakespeare's revisions in many of the plays, including *Romeo and Juliet.*

Irace, Kathleen. *Reforming the "Bad" Quartos.* Newark: University of Delaware Press, 1994. Supports the theory of memorial reconstruction for Q1.

Maguire, Laurie. *Shakespearean Suspect Texts.* Cambridge: Cambridge University Press, 1996. Analyzes all the early quartos of Elizabethan and Jacobean drama and finds few, if any, that can be designated memorial reconstructions, including *Romeo and Juliet.*

Pearlman, E. "Shakespeare at Work: *Romeo and Juliet.*" *English Literary Renaissance* 24 (1994): 315–42. Analyzes Shakespeare's revisions in *Romeo and Juliet* and other plays.

SOURCES AND CONTEXTS

Bullough, Geoffrey, ed. *Narrative and Dramatic Sources of Shakespeare.* 8 vols. London: Routledge; New York: Columbia University Press, 1957–1975. In volume 1, Bullough analyzes Shakespeare's use of his sources and reprints all of Brooke's poem and other suspected sources of *Romeo and Juliet.*

Holmer, Joan Ozark. " 'Draw, if you be men': Saviolo's Significance for *Romeo and Juliet.*" *Shakespeare Quarterly* 45 (1994): 163–89. Mercutio's dueling terms derive from Saviolo's *Practice* (1595).

———. "No 'Vain Fantasy': Shakespeare's Refashioning of Nashe for Dreams and Queen Mab." In *Shakespeare's "Romeo and Juliet": Texts, Contexts, and Interpretation,* ed. Jay L. Halio. Newark: University of Delaware Press, 1995, pp. 49–82. On Shakespeare's debt to Thomas Nashe.

Levenson, Jill. " '*Alla stoccado* carries it away': Codes of Violence in *Romeo and Juliet.*" In *Shakespeare's "Romeo and Juliet": Texts, Contexts, and Interpretation,* ed. Jay L. Halio. Newark: University of Delaware Press, 1995, pp. 83–96. Discusses the background of violence and especially dueling.

Muir, Kenneth. *The Sources of Shakespeare's Plays.* New Haven, Conn.: Yale University Press, 1978. Concise analyses of sources.

GENERAL CRITICISM

Andrews, John F. "Falling in Love: The Tragedy of *Romeo and Juliet.*" In *Classical, Renaissance, and Postmodernist Acts of the Imagination,* ed. Arthur Kinney. Newark: University of Delaware Press, 1996, pp. 177–94. Excellent treatment of the philosophical background to *Romeo and Juliet.*

———, ed. *"Romeo and Juliet": Critical Essays.* New York: Garland, 1993. Contains over two dozen first-rate essays, including excerpts from books by M. M. Mahood, Jack Jorgens, Marianne Novy, Franklin Dickey, and others.

Berry, Ralph. *The Shakespearean Metaphor.* Totowa, N.J.: Rowman and Littlefield, 1978. On Shakespeare's handling of verse.

Brooke, Nicholas. *Shakespeare's Early Tragedies.* London: Methuen, 1968. An excellent, comprehensive analysis of *Romeo and Juliet* in the context of Shakespeare's earlier tragedies.

Charlton, H. B. *Shakespearian Tragedy.* Cambridge: Cambridge University Press, 1948. Discusses *Romeo and Juliet* as an "experimental tragedy."

Clemen, Wolfgang. *The Development of Shakespeare's Imagery.* 2nd ed. London: Methuen, 1977. Not limited to imagery only, but discusses Shakespeare's language more generally.

Cole, Douglas, ed. *Twentieth Century Interpretations of "Romeo and Juliet."* Englewood Cliffs, N.J.: Prentice-Hall, 1970. A good, concise introduction and seven major essays by divers hands, including Harry Levin's "Form and Formality."

Colie, Rosalie L. *Shakespeare's Living Art.* Princeton, N.J.: Princeton University Press, 1974. Contains an excellent section on the language of *Romeo and Juliet.*

Dash, Irene G. *Wooing, Wedding, and Power: Women in Shakespeare's Plays.* New York: Columbia University Press, 1981. An early and perceptive essay on the roles of women in Shakespeare.

Dickey, Franklin M. *Not Wisely but Too Well.* San Marino: Huntington Library, 1957. A book-length study treating many of the important issues, such as the nature of tragedy, in *Romeo and Juliet.*

Evans, Robert O. *The Osier Cage.* Lexington: University of Kentucky Press, 1966. Mainly on Shakespeare's use of rhetorical devices in *Romeo and Juliet.*

Goddard, Harold. *The Meaning of Shakespeare.* Chicago: University of Chicago Press, 1951. One of the best readings of Shakespeare's work, with references to the work of many other writers in Shakespeare's time and ours.

Granville-Barker, Harley. *Prefaces to Shakespeare.* 4 vols. 1930. Reprint, London: Batsford, 1963. Excellent analyses from the point of view of a theater professional.

Halio, Jay L., ed. *Shakespeare's "Romeo and Juliet": Texts, Contexts, and Interpretation.* Newark: University of Delaware Press, 1995. Contains seven important essays by Jill Levenson, Joan Ozark Holmer, Jean-Marie Maguin, François Laroque, and others.

Levin, Harry. "Form and Formality in *Romeo and Juliet.*" *Shakespeare Quarterly* 4 (1960): 3–11; reprinted in *"Romeo and Juliet": Critical Essays,* ed. John F. Andrews. New York: Garland, 1993, pp. 41–53. An insightful essay on the formal aspects of *Romeo and Juliet.*

Mack, Maynard. *Everybody's Shakespeare.* Lincoln: University of Nebraska Press, 1993. The chapter "The Ambiguities of *Romeo and Juliet*" is a superb introduction to the play.

Mahood, M. M. *Shakespeare's Wordplay.* London: Methuen, 1957. The best treatment of Shakespeare's use of puns, quibbles, and other verbal ambiguities.

Nevo, Ruth. *Tragic Form in Shakespeare.* Princeton, N.J.: Princeton University Press, 1972. Contains a chapter with an incisive study of the nature of tragedy in *Romeo and Juliet.*

Porter, Joseph A. *Shakespeare's Mercutio.* Chapel Hill: University of North Carolina Press, 1988. Highly detailed and perceptive historical and critical analyses of Mercutio.

Rabkin, Norman. *Shakespeare and the Common Understanding.* New York: Free Press, 1967. An excellent analysis of *Romeo and Juliet,* exploring the nature of complementarity in the play.

Rose, Mark, ed. *Shakespeare's Early Tragedies.* Englewood Cliffs, N.J.: Prentice-Hall, 1995. Contains essays by Susan Snyder and Coppélia Kahn and excerpts from books by Michael Goldman, Rosalie Colie, and others.

Slater, Ann Pasternak. "Petrarchanism Come True in *Romeo and Juliet*." In *Images of Shake-speare*, ed. Werner Habicht, D. J. Palmer, and Roger Pringle. Newark: University of Delaware Press, 1988, pp. 129–50. Petrarchanism is central to the entire play, as shown in the linguistic texture, narrative structure, dramatic tone, and stage symbol.

Snow, Edward. "Language and Sexual Difference in *Romeo and Juliet*." In *Shakespeare's "Rough Magic*,*"* ed. Peter Erickson and Coppélia Kahn. Newark: University of Delaware Press, 1985, pp. 168–92. A deeply probing essay on the language the lovers use and the way it helps differentiate them.

Snyder, Susan. *The Comic Matrix of Shakespeare's Tragedies*. Princeton, N.J.: Princeton University Press, 1979. Incorporates material from two earlier essays in the larger context of Shakespearean tragedy, including *Othello, Hamlet,* and *King Lear,* as well as *Romeo and Juliet*.

———. "Ideology and the Feud in *Romeo and Juliet*." *Shakespeare Survey* 49 (1996): 87–96. The feud in the play acts as an ideology and offers a model of how ideology works.

Spurgeon, Caroline. *Shakespeare's Imagery and What It Tells Us*. Cambridge: Cambridge University Press, 1935. Describes the function of light and dark imagery in *Romeo and Juliet*.

Wells, Stanley, ed. *"Romeo and Juliet" and Its Afterlife. Shakespeare Survey* 49 (1946). Contains a dozen fine essays on topics ranging from textual studies to language to film productions.

———. *Shakespeare: A Life in Drama*. New York: W. W. Norton, 1995. A complete survey of Shakespeare's work, with a concise and highly perceptive analysis of *Romeo and Juliet*.

PSYCHOANALYTICAL, FEMINIST, AND OTHER CRITICAL APPROACHES

Callaghan, Dympna, Lorraine Helms, and Jyotsna Singh. *The Weyward Sisters: Shake-speare and Feminist Politics*. Oxford: Blackwell, 1994. Contains Callaghan's im-portant essay "The Ideology of Romantic Love: The Case of *Romeo and Juliet*," which treats the problem of historicizing romantic love in the play.

Dusinberre, Juliet. *Shakespeare and the Nature of Women*. 2nd ed. New York: St. Martin's Press, 1996. Originally published twenty years earlier, this is one of the pioneering works in feminist criticism.

Fiedler, Leslie. *The Stranger in Shakespeare*. New York: Stein and Day, 1972. Touches on several myths involved in *Romeo and Juliet*.

Holland, Norman. *Psychoanalysis and Shakespeare*. New York: McGraw-Hill, 1966. Freudian based, but still one of the best introductions to this approach to Shakespeare.

Lenz, Carolyn Ruth Swift, Gayle Greene, and Carol Thomas Neely, eds. *The Woman's Part: Feminist Criticism of Shakespeare*. Urbana: University of Illinois Press, 1980. An excellent anthology of seminal feminist essays, including a good introduction and Coppélia Kahn's "Coming of Age in Verona."

Maguin, Jean-Marie. "Shakespeare, Hypnos, and Thanatos: *Romeo and Juliet* in the Space of Myth." In *Shakespeare's "Romeo and Juliet": Texts, Contexts, and Interpretation*, ed. Jay L. Halio. Newark: University of Delaware Press, 1995, pp. 37–48. Chiefly on the myth of Cupid and Psyche as Shakespeare develops it in *Romeo and Juliet*.

Novy, Marianne. *Love's Argument: Gender Relations in Shakespeare.* Chapel Hill: University of North Carolina Press, 1984. The chapter "Violence, Love, and Gender in *Romeo and Juliet*" probes the feud and the patriarchal structures in the play.

PERFORMANCE CRITICISM AND STAGE HISTORY

Brown, John Russell. *Shakespeare's Plays in Performance.* London: Edward Arnold, 1966. A primer on performance criticism, with a perceptive analysis of Franco Zeffirelli's stage production of *Romeo and Juliet.*

Chambers, E. K. *The Elizabethan Stage.* 4 vols. Oxford: Clarendon Press, 1923. Still the standard reference for information on most aspects of the Elizabethan theater.

Donaldson, Peter S. *Shakespearean Films/Shakespearean Directors.* Boston: Unwin Hyman, 1990. Draws on Zeffirelli's autobiography for insights into his film of *Romeo and Juliet,* especially the interplay of hetero- and homosexual love.

Hogan, Charles Beecher. *Shakespeare in the Theatre, 1701–1800.* 2 vols. Oxford: Clarendon Press, 1952. Provides much useful information on the stage history of Shakespeare's plays for the period.

Jorgens, Jack J. *Shakespeare on Film.* Bloomington: Indiana University Press, 1977. One of the first and most comprehensive books on the subject, with an excellent analysis of the Zeffirelli film.

King, T. J. *Casting of Shakespeare's Plays: London Actors and Their Roles, 1590–1642.* Cambridge: Cambridge University Press, 1992. Examines the composition and disposition of acting companies, including Shakespeare's, and the roles they played.

Levenson, Jill. *Shakespeare in Performance: "Romeo and Juliet."* Manchester: Manchester University Press, 1987. The best concise review of the stage history and major modern productions through the mid-1980s.

Odell, George C. D. *Shakespeare from Betterton to Irving.* 2 vols. New York: Scribner's, 1920. Still a standard reference for the stage history of the eighteenth and nineteenth centuries.

Shattuck, Charles. *Shakespeare on the American Stage.* 2 vols. Washington, D.C.: Folger Library, 1976–1987. The best and most detailed account of Shakespearean productions in the eighteenth and nineteenth centuries in America.

Wells, Stanley. "The Challenges of *Romeo and Juliet.*" *Shakespeare Survey* 49 (1996): 1–14. The challenges are mainly to the actors and directors of this very literary script. Wells also reviews briefly the stage history, especially of modern productions.

Wright, Katherine L. *Shakespeare's "Romeo and Juliet" in Performance: Traditions and Departures.* Lewiston, N.Y.: Edwin Mellen Press, 1997. Surveys performances from Shakespeare's time to the present.

INDEX

About the Author

JAY L. HALIO is Professor of English at the University of Delaware. He is the author of more than 20 books, editions, and collections of essays, not only on Shakespeare and his contemporaries, but also on modern American and British literature. His many publications on Shakespeare include folio and quarto editions of *King Lear* for the *New Cambridge Shakespeare*, an edition of *The Merchant of Venice* for the *New Oxford Shakespeare*, scholarly books on Shakespeare in performance, and numerous articles in journals such as *Shakespeare Quarterly* and *Shakespeare Bulletin*.

ISBN 0-313-30089-5

90000>

EAN

9 780313 300899

HARDCOVER BAR CODE